LIVING AT THE
SPEED OF LIGHT

LIVING AT THE SPEED OF LIGHT

Navigating Life with Bipolar Disorder,
from Depression to Mania and
Everything in Between

KATIE CONIBEAR

Foreword by Calum Harris, Lorraine Gillies and Aditya Sharma,
National Specialist Adolescent Mood Disorders Service,
CNTW NHS Foundation Trust

Jessica Kingsley Publishers
London and Philadelphia

First published in Great Britain in 2021 by Jessica Kingsley Publishers
An Hachette Company

1

The information contained in this book is not intended to replace the services
of trained medical professionals or to be a substitute for medical advice. You
are advised to consult a doctor on any matters relating to your health, and in
particular on any matters that may require diagnosis or medical attention.

Trigger Warning: This book mentions abuse, alcohol, anger issues, anxiety and
panic attacks, Bipolar disorder, car accidents, depression, drugs, hallucinations,
delusions and intrusive thoughts, hospitalization, pregnancy, sex, and suicidal
ideation and thoughts.

A CIP catalogue record for this title is available from the British Library and
the Library of Congress

ISBN 978 1 78775 557 4
eISBN 978 1 78775 558 1

Printed and bound in Great Britain by Clays Ltd

Jessica Kingsley Publishers' policy is to use papers that are natural, renewable
and recyclable products and made from wood grown in sustainable forests.
The logging and manufacturing processes are expected to conform to the
environmental regulations of the country of origin.

Jessica Kingsley Publishers
Carmelite House
50 Victoria Embankment
London EC4Y 0DZ

www.jkp.com

To Jimi, my foundation and my light.
To my family, for their unwavering support and love.

CONTENTS

FOREWORD

As members of the National Specialist Adolescent Mood Disorders Service (SAMS), we took a keen interest in reading *Living at the Speed of Light*. As professionals, we see other young people who have had similar journeys to that described by Katie Conibear in this book. Her story captures the challenges of trying to access the right service at the right time and the stark realities of living with Bipolar. Katie manages to tell her own story in a way that does not feel over-embellished or under-spoken in its message.

This book is a great read for someone recently diagnosed with Bipolar as the narrative is so relatable and accessible due to its honesty. It will help those trying to find some hope that they can still live their life. It will also be of particular interest to family members or friends trying to better understand and empathize with someone they care about, or anyone who would like more knowledge of Bipolar, its impact and how you can start to build a life that is not defined by the diagnosis.

This is an honest and informative story that will impart knowledge whilst keeping you engaged and calling for more.

Calum Harris, Higher Assistant Psychologist, **Lorraine Gillies**, Nurse Practitioner, and **Aditya Sharma**, Clinical Senior Lecturer and Honorary Consultant in Child and Adolescent Psychiatry, National Specialist Adolescent Mood Disorders Service, CNTW NHS Foundation Trust

CHAPTER 1

AN INTRODUCTION TO BIPOLAR DISORDER

At 26, from the outside, it seemed as if I had my life sorted. I had a successful career, an active social life and a steady, loving relationship. Everyone thought I was managing so well, that my life was almost perfect. However, in my head, in my own reality, my life was crumbling.

I'd felt trapped since I was a teenager. I was stuck in this cycle of extreme mood swings, and all I wanted was for it to stop. In the months before, I'd been manic and out of control. I didn't sleep and spent money impulsively, racking up debt. I caused two car accidents and acted on impulse. All the time, I was extremely intense and talkative, or angry and irrational. Now, vicious voices in my head shouted and screamed at me to end it all. I couldn't see a way forward, and I felt eerily calm about the idea of taking my own life. Slowly, things changed for me. Over the years, I learned to manage what I found out was Bipolar disorder. I read up on the condition and discovered practical techniques to help me cope, and later thrive.

This is my experience and I'll be exploring it throughout the book. My aim here is to explain Bipolar disorder, to provide practical tips and advice, and to really get down to the nitty gritty of the illness. We could all do with a real no-nonsense guide, to understand the condition, support someone or feel less alone.

SO, WHAT IS BIPOLAR DISORDER REALLY?

Bipolar disorder is characterized by extreme lows and extreme highs. To put it simply, this means extreme mood swings. Lows can lead to suicidal depression, and highs result in hypomania or mania. In the past, Bipolar was referred to as manic depression. Bipolar is difficult to diagnose, as it affects each individual differently. For example, not everyone has extreme mania, which can result in reckless behaviour, delusions and hallucinations. I'll explain the differences between hypomania and mania later on, in Chapter 3.

Here are some important stats to remember (I bloody love stats), which explain just how hard it is to receive a correct diagnosis of Bipolar disorder:

- In the UK, 2 per cent of the population have Bipolar (McManus *et al.* 2016).
- In the US, 4.4 per cent of people are affected by Bipolar at some point in their lives (National Institute of Mental Health 2017).
- It can take on average 10.5 years to receive a correct diagnosis (Ghaemi 2001).
- Individuals with Bipolar are misdiagnosed, on average, 3.5 times (Ghaemi 2001).

WHERE IT ALL STARTED

At 14 years old, my life changed. I had no problems at school, I wasn't being bullied and I was a high achiever. At home, I lived in a stable, caring environment. Despite this, I became severely depressed. I became a school refuser. I'd lock myself in the bathroom and threaten to hurt myself. It had been building for months, but I didn't realize what was happening to me. I became more withdrawn; I didn't understand why I felt so numb and worthless, or why I no longer cared if I was alive. I missed six months of school. During that time, I saw a psychologist to whom I felt I could speak openly about my feelings. I wanted to get better, which was vital to the process.

Yet something strange happened when I returned to school. I became unbelievably confident, loud and brash. Everyone began to notice, but I felt as if nothing was wrong. My family thought:

'It's just teenage hormones, right?'

I was feeling the best I'd ever been.

After school, at the age of 18, I decided to go to university, and that's where my behaviour started to really unravel. I showed signs of mania. I was hardly sleeping and was partying constantly. I didn't realize what was going on and felt incredible. Everyone around me this time thought:

'She's just embracing the university lifestyle!'

Without warning, my mood crashed. I hid in my room, scared to bump into anyone. I couldn't manage the idea of having to explain why my behaviour had changed so drastically. No one else knew why, so how could I? I ended up dropping out of university in the first year, desperately depressed.

Because I experienced mania, I was eventually (after a very, very long time) diagnosed with Bipolar type 1. Let's look at the different types of Bipolar.

TYPES OF BIPOLAR

Bipolar 1 is usually diagnosed if you've experienced:

- mania (at least one episode) that lasts longer than a week
- episodes of depression (though not everyone experiences these).

Bipolar 2 is diagnosed if you've experienced:

- a bout of severe depression, at least once in your life
- a period of hypomania.

Cyclothymia is diagnosed if you've had:

- both hypomania and depression for over two years or more
- symptoms that don't meet the criteria for a diagnosis of Bipolar 1 or 2 but still have a serious impact on your life.

There are two other terms that you may come across:

- **Rapid cycling.** Sounds random, right? And no, it's not cycling incredibly fast on a pedal bike. If you're told you have rapid cycling, it means your mood states fluctuate in quick succession. Usually, you'll be told you have this if you've had four or more depressive, manic or mixed episodes in a year. It's not an actual type of Bipolar disorder, yet. More research needs to be done to get a better understanding of what rapid cycling is.

- **Mixed episodes.** Also referred to as 'mixed states'. This is when you experience mania (the highs) and depression in very quick succession. It might get to the point that you feel both at the same time. It can be extremely challenging to manage and to keep your emotions in check.

MY LIFE BEFORE DIAGNOSIS

My life became a cycle of churning moods, from ecstatically high to incredibly low. I felt as if I was completely and utterly controlled by them. I studied childcare at college, but became angry and combative towards my lecturers – a symptom of mania or hypomania. I ended up walking out in a fit of rage, just two months before graduating. Somehow, with a stroke of luck, the same day I walked out, I found an apprenticeship in childcare.

Again, I became depressed and for the first time started taking antidepressants. Instead of stabilizing me, they made me feel superhuman and I would stop taking them, convincing myself everything was back to normal.

Sometimes, as a side effect, antidepressants can cause mania or hypomania. It's best to see a doctor and explain what's happening. Under supervision, if you stop taking the antidepressants, you can see if the mania or hypomania persists. This might give an explanation as to whether or not you actually have Bipolar disorder. Antidepressants can be used as a treatment for Bipolar, but alongside other medications such as mood stabilizers. I'll go into more detail about the different types of medication in the next chapter.

I had two serious relationships that both ended for the same reason: they couldn't deal with how much I would change month by month. They never knew which Katie they were going to get.

The breakdown of these relationships led me to believe I was a broken person, intrinsically flawed, and would never find happiness. Then I started seeing Jimi. We clicked instantly. He had, and still does have, a calming influence on me. He doesn't overreact at my sometimes bizarre behaviour. We moved in together and I started a job as a family worker for children's services at the local council. I was passionate about this work and making a difference to people's lives.

People would tell me that I seemed so happy and contented, but inside I was struggling. Doctors didn't understand why my physical health was suffering, or why I kept coming back depressed and exhausted. Family and friends would say to me:

'How are you so tired all the time, you're only in your mid 20s?!'

There is evidence of a link between mental illnesses like Bipolar and our physical health. Often with Bipolar, we become rundown or experience burnout. Then we get physically ill. What happens is that we're not looking after ourselves properly, either because we're too depressed to eat and sleep properly, or because we're manic or hypomanic and don't feel the need to eat or sleep. Eating and sleeping are pretty important (obviously) as they both help to keep us healthy and repair the body. So being mentally ill compromises our immune system, and we fall prey to illness.

THE VOICES

The voices in my head grew louder and more intrusive. It was a sign of psychosis, but it was another symptom of Bipolar I didn't understand. This time, I knew something was wrong, but I was in denial. When I was depressed, I would lie in bed, begging the voices to go away. Sometimes they would urge me to be more impulsive, more reckless. These voices filled me with confidence and a surge of adrenaline. They became a major part of my life and I missed them when they were gone.

This experience, along with an intense period of hyperactive behaviour, led me to the lowest I'd ever felt. I had to leave the job I loved, and I became suicidal. It was as if my life had come full circle, and I felt like that frightened 14-year-old again. I was exhausted from spending over a decade in a battle with my mind. I felt that there were no answers and no hope.

SO WHERE DOES BIPOLAR COME FROM?

No one really knows the cause of Bipolar disorder. There are a few different factors that, combined, increase your chances of developing the illness. Researchers suggest causes range from physical, environmental and social. Those of us with Bipolar can look back and identify one or more of these influences in our lives.

CHILDHOOD TRAUMA
There are medical experts who feel that trauma we may have experienced as children can result in us having Bipolar disorder later on. This could include:

- physical abuse
- sexual abuse
- emotional abuse
- neglect
- a bereavement of someone you are close to
- a traumatic situation.

Emotional distress can have a significant impact on a child, and its effects can follow them into adulthood. Experts believe this could take the form of developing Bipolar disorder. Research suggests that trauma in childhood can play a part in how we deal with emotions. You may find it difficult to regulate or keep in check your emotions if you've been through distressing experiences as a child.

STRESSFUL LIFE EVENTS

Everyone goes through stressful situations, but some people can look back and pinpoint the beginnings of Bipolar to a stressful time in their life. It could be an unexpected bereavement, being involved in an accident, the end of a relationship, or living in poverty. Why do some people develop Bipolar due to stress and others don't? Well, it may be because of a predisposition to the condition due to brain chemistry or genetic inheritance.

BRAIN CHEMISTRY

Neurotransmitters are basically messengers in your brain that send chemicals around it. But the human brain is so complicated and intricate that no one knows for sure exactly how these neurotransmitters work. The idea is that people with Bipolar disorder have neurotransmitters that don't work the way they should. The reasoning behind this is that psychiatric medications are used to treat Bipolar disorder and, in most people, there is a clear improvement in symptoms. However, are these neurotransmitters being faulty a cause or just another symptom of the disorder? Neuroscientists are constantly learning more and more about how our brains work, so it is hoped that in the not too distant future we'll have a clearer answer!

GENETIC INHERITANCE

It's very likely that if you have Bipolar disorder, someone in your family has it too. There's a suggestion that the disorder runs in families. They might not have a diagnosis, but a family member may have noticed they experience the symptoms. For instance, my Dad believes his biological mother had Bipolar disorder. I never met her, as my Dad was adopted, but her behaviour that led to him being taken into care shows signs of the illness. At the time, in the 1950s, people were less likely to be diagnosed with a mental illness. There was less understanding and awareness, so it's possible she was unwell. Although there are often shared diagnoses in families, there isn't evidence of a specific gene that can be passed on. However, anecdotal evidence for many families shows there is a link.

For me, it's physical. I think a combination of brain chemistry and genetic inheritance have caused me to have Bipolar. I never experienced childhood trauma, and although I went through stressful life events as a child, I don't feel they were severe enough to trigger the illness. We're all different, and all have our own stories to tell, including what caused our mental illness.

HOW DO YOU ACTUALLY GET A DIAGNOSIS OF BIPOLAR?

It isn't something your local general practitioner or family doctor can diagnose. They may have an inkling that you have the condition, but they can't make a formal diagnosis or start your treatment. For this, you'll have to see a psychiatrist. They specialize in diagnosing and treating people with mental illness, so have a wealth of knowledge and experience in this area that a family doctor just doesn't have.

To get an appointment with a psychiatrist, you first have to be referred. This might be through another doctor, a therapist, a social worker or a psychologist.

ASSESSMENT

Before you can be diagnosed, you'll have to go through a psychiatric assessment.

You may be given 'homework' before your assessment, such as:

- keeping a mood journal or filling out a mood tracker each day. This will show the doctor if you're currently experiencing drastic mood swings.
- writing a chronology, from the first time you showed symptoms. This will give the psychiatrist an insight into how many episodes of mania, hypomania or depression you have experienced.
- thinking about what you want to say and explain, and making notes to bring with you.

During the assessment, the psychiatrist may want to talk through the journal and chronology with you, to get a better picture of your moods and the effect they have had on your daily life. They may ask questions that feel a little awkward or personal, such as about drug and alcohol use, your sex life, your finances and relationships, all of which can be affected by Bipolar symptoms.

To give the psychiatrist even more insight into your behaviour and actions, it's a good idea to take a close family member or friend with you to the assessment. Take a person that you trust and who knows you well. For instance, I took my Mum along to my assessment. As I'd been showing signs of Bipolar since I was 14, she was best placed to describe any symptoms I'd been displaying. This person doesn't need to understand what Bipolar is, but rather they are there to provide evidence of when you've been feeling very depressed, or when they've noticed you've been acting strangely or erratically. The psychiatrist may ask them questions about you, but don't be offended if they start talking about you while you're in the room!

Depending on the evidence they have, and the psychiatrist, they may diagnose you at the assessment or write to you or ring a few days afterwards. It can be a long appointment (mine lasted two hours) and it will be emotionally draining. Make sure to schedule time off work or school after the assessment if you need to. Everyone should go and treat themselves after something as intense as that!

'HOW DO I APPROACH A DOCTOR IF I THINK I MIGHT HAVE BIPOLAR?'

KEEP A MOOD DIARY

This is the main thing I wish I'd done before seeing my doctor. Keeping a mood diary for a few months will give them a picture of how much you're struggling and the stark contrast in your moods. It can be difficult to explain how much your moods are impacting your life, and a mood diary is a definitive way to show them this. You may be thinking two to three months is a long time to wait before seeing a doctor, but, believe me, three months is better than waiting another three years or longer for a diagnosis. Entries don't have to be long. You can make bullet points explaining your mood that day. Bullet points will also make it easier for the doctor to read through.

ASK FOR A DOUBLE APPOINTMENT

Most doctor's surgeries will have the option of making a double appointment. These are reserved for people with more than one ailment to discuss or those with more complex needs. An average appointment is only ten minutes and this can go by in a flash if you're feeling mentally unwell and struggling to explain yourself. You may feel rushed and forget what you wanted to say. Giving a clearer picture of your moods is a vital step in receiving a diagnosis.

WRITE DOWN WHAT YOU WANT TO SAY

Feeling mentally unwell can make us forgetful and anxious. It stops us from explaining ourselves fully. You can't show a doctor Bipolar; unfortunately, they can only rely on what we say. Write down what you want to tell your doctor before the appointment. It will make it clearer in your mind what you need to explain and highlight important points. Take it with you and refer to it if you can't remember what you were going to say. If you're feeling extremely anxious or upset and don't think you can speak clearly enough, give your notes to the doctor to read for themselves.

TAKE SOMEONE WITH YOU

Bringing along a partner, family member or close friend will take the pressure off you during the appointment. Not only will having someone there who knows you well, and what you're struggling with, provide you with much needed support, but they can corroborate your symptoms. A doctor will be more likely to take your concerns seriously if someone with you is agreeing that they've witnessed your extreme moods and unusual behaviours. Their insights may provide information that you can't, such as how your moods and behaviours are affecting those around you.

BE ASSERTIVE

This is a difficult one, but something that I feel is important. You know how you're feeling and how your symptoms are affecting you, and you need to make this clear. Often those with Bipolar disorder, before they are diagnosed, are misdiagnosed with depression and anxiety. In a short appointment, a doctor may assess you as having depression, as it's the most obvious answer and much more common. If you feel something else is happening, and you're struggling with hypomanic, manic, psychotic or other symptoms, you need to tell the doctor. Being assertive doesn't mean you have to be aggressive or confrontational. It means making your points confidently and articulately.

A good doctor will take the time to speak to you and check your medical history, which may highlight patterns of earlier mental illness that link to signs of Bipolar disorder.

CHAPTER 2

I'VE BEEN DIAGNOSED, SO WHAT DO I DO NOW?

Although my diagnosis didn't solve everything, it showed me I wasn't flawed; I was ill. Receiving any Bipolar diagnosis is a difficult and confusing time. It can leave you feeling emotionally raw and incredibly vulnerable. Surround yourself with supportive people during this time. I'd advise that you don't hide the fact you have Bipolar from the people closest to you; it can be a big deal to tell people, but it's more than likely they'll want to be there for you.

For me, I felt a mixture of emotions: 10am on 13 December 2012 was a life-changing moment. I was diagnosed with Bipolar type 1. I had had a psychiatric assessment at Prospect Park Hospital. I sat with the psychiatrist for two hours, unpicking my past. I'd been asked to bring a diary of past events and to try to track my moods since I was a teenager, from the first time I'd found myself depressed. I tracked from the year 2000 to the present day, and it became clear that there was a pattern of depressive and manic episodes. Looking around the room, it seemed strange that such a drab, lifeless place was the setting of one of the most important, life-altering events I had ever been through. It was a typical NHS (National Health Service) office with very little character, a shared room for various staff.

The most shocking part of my appointment was the assuredness of the diagnosis given. After so many years of frustration at my ever-changing behaviour and painful bouts of depression, I had begun to accept it was 'just me', that I would have to continually reinvent myself and start over as the vicious cycle of extreme moods I was trapped in moulded my ambitions and relationships. I'd started to believe I was a lost cause and there was no answer to my increasingly erratic and bizarre behaviour.

I had been through so many doctors' appointments, with their own theories and remedies. Cognitive behavioural therapy twice, antidepressants, citalopram and fluoxetine, prescribed. Countless blood tests with all my problems attributed to a physical problem, which would then all come back negative or normal. I was convinced on a regular basis that I had chronic fatigue syndrome as my energy levels would plummet so drastically. Then there were the doctors who thought a few simple changes would solve everything, or I could think myself to a more balanced life. If I had enough will to change my moods, I could.

'Have you tried an exclusion diet?'

'Are you getting enough exercise?'

'A bath, hot drink and a good book before bed will do you wonders.'

Why would I see a doctor if I hadn't tried these methods already? It was patronizing and frankly dangerous advice to hand out to someone so obviously struggling. Over the years, I've had crying fits and full-blown temper tantrums following yet another appointment filled with the same questions and advice. Another furrowed brow and bewildered looks would leave me with yet another question mark hanging over me. So you can imagine my shock when faced with an actual diagnosis.

I cried after the appointment. I felt a mixture of relief, fear and anger – relief that I could move forward, that I wasn't stuck on a waiting list anymore and that decisions had been made, that someone had not only listened to me, but had given me some affirmation of how unwell I'd been, and how difficult it must have been for me.

I felt fear for the future. I knew there was no quick fix but that this was a lifelong condition to which I had to adjust. I was concerned about what this meant for my relationships with my partner, my family and friends. And anger. The psychiatrist had stated it took, 'on average ten years for a patient to be diagnosed with Bipolar'.

I left the hospital thinking that all it needed was for one doctor in the past 12 years to have taken the initiative and asked me a couple more questions – something along the lines of: had I ever had extreme mood swings and did I ever act out of character during these times? It would have taken five minutes of their time.

I felt anger that it had taken until I was 27, and 13 years of pain and suffering, to finally have a diagnosis. So many years of my life felt wasted, as I had dragged myself through horrific bouts of depression. I had self-destructed countless times as my manic episodes had caused my behaviour to spiral out of control. I was broke, in debt and unemployed. I wanted to scream and yell at all the doctors who had misdiagnosed me over the years. I felt that someone had to be held accountable for everything I'd missed out on in my teens and for most of my 20s. There was no one, though, that I could single out and blame; it was just the way it went for many people with Bipolar. I had to let it go. For my own piece of mind, my health, I had to let it go.

When the anger subsided, I realized how this label I'd been given explained my erratic behaviour. It gave meaning to my partner, family and friends for my sometimes bizarre actions. Instead of recoiling from this label, they were willing to listen and wanted to understand more about the disorder. I feared that such a diagnosis would scare my family and friends. It didn't. This reaction filled me with the confidence to be able to tell more and more people about my diagnosis. When asked why I wasn't working, or why I was ill, I was always able to be truthful.

Being labelled was a release. No longer did I feel weighed down with the burden of knowing that I was ill, but not understanding what it was. I could prove that I wasn't attention-seeking when I was suicidal, or that I would magically just get over what I was feeling. I was armed with knowledge, and I could now educate myself and learn how to combat and find some relief from this illness.

We all process news differently. Being diagnosed at first can almost feel like a bereavement. There is a crushing weight that you'll have this diagnosis probably for the rest of your life. It's a huge life change that can't be underestimated. Take care of yourself, and allow time to get your head around the diagnosis. Remember, you are the expert on you. Ask your psychiatrist as many questions as you can about Bipolar disorder, and use that knowledge to decide what treatment will work best for you. A good psychiatrist will discuss all the options with you, and provide you with the pros and cons. They might be a medical professional, but you should always have the final decision about treatment.

Eventually, I found a mix of medications that worked for me and I began to experience times when I felt stable.

MEDICATIONS

First of all, I am not a medical professional. The following is a list of different medications that can help with the symptoms of Bipolar. It has been reviewed by medical professionals, but please remember that the information contained in this book is not a substitute for their advice and support.

LITHIUM

Lithium is usually used in the long term, to reduce the symptoms of mania, depression and suicidal feelings. It's heavy stuff, so you'll need to have regular blood tests and a general check-up at the doctor's (a bit like an MOT or service for your car). If the levels are wrong, then it can have an impact on your physical health, so it's really important to go to these appointments.

ANTIPSYCHOTICS

These are prescribed if you've experienced psychotic symptoms, such as hearing or seeing things that aren't really there (hallucinations) or believing wild ideas (delusions). This may happen during severe episodes of mania or severe depression. But if you're prescribed them when you don't experience psychosis, don't freak out. The side effects can be less of a pain to live with, so if you've had problems with other medications, you might be offered them. The National Institute for Health and Care Excellence (NICE) creates the guidelines for treatment and recommends taking for Bipolar disorder:

- Risperidone
- Olanzapine
- Quetiapine
- Haloperidol.

If you're given an antipsychotic and it doesn't work, as you can see, there are other options. Lithium alongside an antipsychotic might be offered. Again, as with Lithium, you'll need to go to regular check-ups with your doctor.

ANTICONVULSANTS

Don't let the name fool you. Anticonvulsants are often used in Bipolar disorder as a mood stabilizer. If, for whatever reason, Lithium doesn't work or is unsuitable for you, this might be the way forward. However, some of these medications can cause problems in pregnancy, and you may be advised to use alternatives. Again, NICE recommends any of these three medications to treat Bipolar disorder:

- Lamotrigine
- Carbamazepine
- Valproate.

ANTIDEPRESSANTS

As I mentioned in the previous chapter, antidepressants on their own can cause hypomanic or manic episodes. However, in some circumstances, you may well be offered antidepressants. Usually for Bipolar disorder, it would be an SSRI (selective serotonin re-uptake inhibitor). This would be prescribed alongside another type of Bipolar medication from the lists above.

Remember to always follow your doctor's advice and take the correct dosage – and don't suddenly stop taking them! Withdrawal is a bitch and can cause you to feel very unwell. I have the memory of a fish (which is a common symptom of Bipolar, but we'll talk about that later) and was forgetting to take my meds, only taking them every other day. It meant they weren't doing their job and I often felt physically ill and rundown. So what do you do to remind yourself?

- Put an alarm reminder on your phone and set it for the same time every day.
- Download a medication reminder on your phone.
- Buy a pill box with a different section for each day of the week. This will help if you often forget whether you've taken your medications!
- Talk to your doctor about the best time to take your meds; maybe it works better for you to take them all at once, in the morning or evening. Always consult your doctor before doing this, because some medications can make you feel either drowsy or alert.

ALCOHOL = BAD

You know those warnings on your medications that say:

'Do not consume alcohol while taking this medication.'

Well, with the above, they really mean it. I think many of us have read these warnings and thought, stuff it, I'm not giving up alcohol! We think we will be the exception. Nothing will go wrong. Those warnings are just there to scare us. With Bipolar medications, it's not an exaggeration to say it's a catastrophically bad idea. Believe me, I've tried it.

To put it simply, alcohol 'cancels out' the effects of the medication. A psychiatrist once told me, after I told him how much I would drink in a week:

'You might as well not bother taking your medication.'

Alcohol is a depressant, so often after a heavy weekend of drinking I'd be feeling unbelievably low. I'd have palpitations, have no motivation and feel desperate and alone. I'd feel this way sometimes for weeks. It would often be a trigger for depression, hypomania or mania. What I've learned with alcohol is that the good times you have are just simply not worth it.

THERAPY

There are quite a few types of therapy that can help with Bipolar symptoms. Talking therapies, for instance, are usually offered during a depressive episode because they address negative thought patterns. When you're in mania or hypomania, it's less likely you'll be offered therapy at that time. Because we often feel elated and that nothing is wrong, therapy doesn't exactly sound as if it's needed! You'll probably be offered medication, and then therapy at a later date. Not all types of therapy work for everyone. For instance, I didn't get on with cognitive behavioural therapy, but everyone is different and this could end up being beneficial for you.

GROUP OR SOLO THERAPY
You may be offered therapy as part of a group, or one to one with a psychologist or therapist. This could depend on the budgets of your local authority or hospital, waiting times for individual therapy, and what you've decided with your psychiatrist would work well for you. Group therapy has the added benefit of getting to know others with the condition. If you've just been diagnosed, this can help you feel less alone and isolated. Sharing stories, tips and advice can be as beneficial as the therapy itself. However, going solo could be a better option if you find group situations stressful. You might feel you can concentrate more

fully one on one, or there might be topics you want to talk about that you're uncomfortable sharing with a group.

COGNITIVE BEHAVIOURAL THERAPY

Cognitive behavioural therapy (CBT) is a talking therapy that focuses on how your thoughts and feelings impact on your behaviour. It looks at negative patterns of thinking and how you can change the way you think and find a way out of these patterns.

INTERPERSONAL THERAPY

Instead of looking at patterns of thoughts like CBT, interpersonal therapy focuses on how our relationships affect our feelings and behaviour and how Bipolar can have a negative impact on our relationships.

ENHANCED RELAPSE PREVENTION/INDIVIDUAL OR GROUP PSYCHOEDUCATION

Led by a trained therapist, this type of therapy helps you learn coping strategies to prevent relapses and educates us on what is effective and what can trigger an episode. In groups or one to one, this therapy helps us to build up our knowledge of Bipolar and how we ourselves can manage it.

BEHAVIOURAL COUPLES THERAPY

As Bipolar can affect our relationships, it might be helpful to have couples therapy. It can help resolve issues that have arisen because of our behaviours, and give our partner a better understanding of Bipolar.

FAMILY-FOCUSED THERAPY

Like couples therapy, you'll work as a family to build communication skills and learn about different behaviours together.

WHAT'S AVAILABLE DURING A CRISIS?

A crisis is when an episode of depression, hypomania or mania makes you feel extremely unwell. You might be suicidal, have made plans to hurt yourself and even tried to make an attempt on your life. It might be you can't 'come down' from mania, or depression is lasting for a long time, even with treatment. This means you need help urgently, and there are a few options you can take during a crisis:

- Go to the accident and emergency department at your local hospital.
- Seek out home support available in your area, such as a crisis resolution and home treatment team.
- Seek hospital admission from your psychiatrist.

If you feel you're not able to do any of these, there are helplines available, which are included at the end of the book.

TREATMENT IN HOSPITAL

Sometimes to keep us safe, it's best to have a stay in hospital. If we're at a high risk of hurting ourselves, because of self-harming or planning on acting on suicidal thoughts, and there isn't a way for us to be safe and properly treated at home, we may be admitted. This is especially so if our current treatment isn't working and we need to be monitored more closely. If mania or hypomania puts us at risk, or we're more likely to find ourselves in a dangerous situation that could hurt us or others, again hospital admission might be the right way to go.

It can be a big step to admit you might need treatment in hospital. It's a daunting prospect and can make you feel afraid and anxious about such an unknown experience. There are many pros and cons to hospital admission, and it's always a good idea to talk to people you trust about all of them before you decide.

THE PROS

- Treatment, such as a range of different therapies and medications, will be available.
- It can be a break from everyday life. It might help you 'reset' if you're away from stress in your life, work and family.
- There will be support from trained staff that you just can't access when you're at home.
- When we're very unwell, it's hard to keep to a routine. Hospitals give structure to every day.
- It stops us from being isolated, as we may be when we're ill and living at home.

THE CONS

- Too much structure might mean you can't do what you want to do all of the time.
- You might feel bored or just not enjoy the activities that are on offer.
- Family and friends can't pop in to see you when they feel like it, and you might not be able to leave whenever you want.
- Some hospitals have mixed wards that might make you feel uncomfortable.
- You may be held in hospital under the Mental Health Act (1983), which is also known as being sectioned. This means having treatment without your agreement. This may happen if you try to leave when you're very unwell.
- In the UK especially, there is a shortage of beds, so you may have to stay in a hospital a long way from home.

For me, hospital wasn't the right choice. When I was severely depressed, I spoke to family, my partner and my psychiatrist about hospitalization. Even though I was suicidal, and the depression would not lift after months and months, deep down I didn't want to go into hospital. On the one hand, I felt as if I needed a break from everything. The drudgery of daily life wasn't helping and I felt like a burden on my partner and family. On the other hand, I'm a very stubborn person and hate being told what to do and when – for example, I went to Scouts once as a kid and thought:

'Why is everyone telling me what to do? This is just like school!'

I couldn't stand being ordered around and having structured activities. Give me an authoritative regime, and it's a guarantee I'll rebel. I never went back. I didn't even get a badge. I knew in hospital there would be structure and routine, and I'd be encouraged to get involved. I felt that my personality would clash with the daily hospital routine and I'd eventually resent being there. It's not for everyone, but for others it can be hugely beneficial. We're all different, and how we go about finding treatment in difficult times is, of course, going to be different too. The most important thing is to stay safe. If hospitalization is going to keep you safe, or you or your loved ones feel you can't keep yourself safe at home, then it might be the best option.

BETTER TIMES

Jimi and I got married in 2015. He is compassionate, caring and the most supportive person in my life. I feel truly lucky to have found someone who has taken my illness in their stride, and been able to see beyond it and see me as a person. With his support, I've been able to accept my diagnosis.

I started writing a blog, *Stumbling Mind*, about my mental illness journey and Bipolar. I've found it really therapeutic. This led me to pursuing a career as a freelance writer, which I adore. I'm not afraid to be open with others and have had so much support from family, friends and complete strangers.

Although I can't work full-time, writing has given me a renewed sense of purpose. I've learned that although I've had to make adjustments to my life, I can still live well. Bipolar doesn't control me. I'm more than a diagnosis.

Bipolar is a lifelong condition, but it can be managed with the correct treatment. I still suffer from difficult episodes of mania and depression, but I'm continually learning to educate myself and manage the condition. I no longer feel frightened and alone, but instead I feel in control and positive about the future.

CHAPTER 3

MANIA AND HYPOMANIA

Living at the Speed of Light

'I'm sorry, you can't have Bipolar – you seem so nice!'

Exclaimed a friend of a friend who I'd been introduced to and started chatting with. Someone who had known me for all of an hour. What she was trying to say was that I was too nice to ever be manic.

'Well, I'm not going to suddenly attack you, or go on a rampage through the high street, if that's what you think Bipolar is.'

I'm pretty upfront about living with Bipolar, and conversations like this are not new. I have my patter all sorted and ready to go. The idea that Bipolar – and, as an extension, mania – makes you a bad person is strange to me. Mania, in fact, makes me more likeable – gregarious, the life of the party. I want to talk to everybody and they want to talk to me. It doesn't make me a vile, evil person. It's true that mania can turn. It can make me incredibly angry. I've lashed out at people who I care about deeply. This doesn't make me a nasty person. I always say that the reasons for my behaviour at these times aren't an excuse, but more of an explanation. I apologize and never rely on the fact I have Bipolar to get out of an apology.

I often describe mania as a faulty light switch. You turn on the light, a stark light, a bare bulb with no lampshade. It makes the people around you squint when they look directly at it. It's glaringly bright and a touch uncomfortable. You flick the switch to turn off the light, but it won't work. The light is stuck permanently on, until you can find a way to fix it.

I really do feel that I'm moving at the speed of light. It's almost as if flashes strike across my vision. They streak past at a ferocious pace and feel endless. I'll feel as if I'm in a tireless race in my own mind. There's so much to do. There's so much to experience. My thoughts are constantly being cut down. Another competing idea emerges. Then there's another, and another. These bright flashes in my mind feel so vivid I could almost reach out and touch them.

Mania for me is:

- reckless, dangerous driving
- spending masses of money I don't have
- an irrational, intense anger towards everything and everyone
- believing I can rule the world, and that anything is possible
- paranoia following me everywhere, whispering in my ear
- hearing voices that boost my self-belief.

SO WHAT IS MANIA REALLY?

Let's start with the two main types: mania and hypomania.

Hypomania begins with accelerated speech, where you talk very fast and people find it difficult to keep up with what you're

38

saying. You'll feel as if you don't need to sleep or eat as much as you normally do. Thoughts are uncontrollable and constant. Hypomania, although less extreme than full-blown mania, can be just as damaging and self-destructive.

With mania, your judgement may become impaired and you start to act impulsively. The most serious aspects of mania are characterized by a complete lack of control and putting yourself in dangerous situations, as well as delusional thinking (believing wild ideas about yourself or others) or hallucinations (seeing, hearing, feeling things that are not really there).

Mania and hypomania can be accompanied by depression, during what's called a mixed episode.

People with Bipolar type 1 are more likely to develop mania, while those with Bipolar type 2 will experience mostly hypomania.

The most important thing to remember is that mania and hypomania *are far more than just being happy*. Mania is tricky. It's sneaky. It creeps up on you without you realizing. One minute you're feeling productive and happy, then a few weeks later you find yourself in full-blown mania. In the midst of everyday life, it's easy to lose sight of your moods when you live with Bipolar.

If it isn't addressed and treated, hypomania can easily turn into something more severe, and you can find yourself in the throes of mania. Mania doesn't always feel good. You're not always ecstatic and the life of the party. It can be as self-destructive and life-threatening as severe depression. It's hypomania but brighter and louder, so much so it's as if your senses are overloaded.

IS IT A GOOD MOOD OR IS IT HYPOMANIA?

The problem I have over and over again is being able to tell whether I'm in a good mood or in the early stages of hypomania.

I have been in a hypomanic state when family and friends believed I was happy and just in a good mood. What they didn't see was that I was constantly 'on', like that light with a faulty switch I mentioned earlier. It's a dangerous time, as relentless energy pushes me further and to do more and more. I can't sleep or eat because my mind is desperately active; it needs to be satiated with action and excitement.

Hypomania is the lesser extreme of mania. You have unbounded self-confidence and you feel constantly restless and itching to start that new project you've been dreaming about. A good mood and hypomania can present as extremely similar to an outsider and even to the person experiencing them.

It can be irritating and unpleasant, such as when you're trying to sleep and it's 3 in the morning, but your body is constantly in an awkward position, and you can never seem to get comfortable. I feel like raging and screaming because of the pressure building inside my head, but there's no release valve. It's not anything like 'feeling good'.

A TRIP FUELLED BY MANIA

When I have to explain mania to someone new, I often talk about a trip I took to Japan. It encompasses many of the aspects of mania that I'll explain in more detail in this chapter. I went alone, impulsively booking the flight and expensive hotels.

I would walk around Shinjuku, a district of Tokyo, at night. The lights in this district were bright and vivid, brimming with images and pictures accosting the senses from every direction. People bustled about, swarming at the entrances of the subway, shopping malls and skyscrapers. All of this was a reflection of the mania in my mind. I couldn't get enough of the energy the city was expelling, I fed off it. I would stay out until the early hours of the morning, roaming the area looking for interesting bars to drink in and people to meet. I partied with complete strangers through the night, not thinking about the consequences of my actions. Again, everything went on the credit cards – the hotels, the trips, nights out, presents for friends and family.

I play-acted while I was in Japan, pretending to be someone different each day. One day I would be the average tourist, going on scheduled trips to Kyoto or Mount Fuji and the surrounding countryside. The next day I was the fangirl, head to toe in cute kawaii-style clothing, heading for the Ghibli Museum, full of treats from the animation studio. The nights I would spend looking for somewhere fun, and end up in karaoke bars singing my heart out. I would always find people to talk to, my manic self giving me an ease of conversation I would have otherwise lacked. I invited men from these bars back to my hotel room. I was in a relationship at the time. My partner was back in England but I knew what I wanted to happen. My judgement was clouded. My mind wasn't weighing up the positives and negatives as it should have been. My conscience didn't have a glaring neon sign up in capital letters saying NO!

One night, before sundown, I bought a bottle of Yamazaki whiskey and drank the entirety of it as I watched the sunset from my hotel room. At the time, I was hearing voices, and I spoke to them as I drank. They were loud and intruding, but I didn't mind.

THE 'SOMETIMES' POSITIVE

Mania and hypomania present differently in each individual; however, there are a number of shared behaviours and actions that I'll touch on in this chapter. I always think it's good to start with the positives. No one wants to hear the bad news first, do they?

CREATIVITY

Creativity, productiveness and ideas, ideas, ideas! Mania gives me those eureka light-bulb moments during an episode.

The creativity comes in many forms:

- You might feel the urge to write a novel (and have the self-belief it *will* be a bestseller).
- You might dig out your paints and pens if you have an artistic flair.
- For the entrepreneurial type, it might be the seed of an idea for a new business venture.

This all sounds wonderful right now, doesn't it?! I've truly had some of my best ideas and been the most productive I've ever been during an episode of mania or hypomania.

What I've listed above is not mutually exclusive. In the midst of mania, I've had ideas for all three of these at once. My head will feel full to the brim with ideas that I'm convinced have never before been thought of, are never-to-be-repeated nuggets of gold. Mania can give you normally unattainable masses of confidence and self-esteem. When this translates into creativity, your ideas become an unstoppable force. However – and I can't stress this enough – *it doesn't suddenly turn you into a creative genius*. It would be incredible if it did, but we can't all be like Stephen Fry, unfortunately. Often, that creativity can become overwhelming.

Mania is all-encompassing. Your creative ideas can take hold of you until you can't focus or think about anything else. You become completely and entirely obsessed. I've spent days and nights sitting writing hunched over my laptop or notebook. I've gone without sleep for three nights in a row because I just *had* to get out all these ideas circling my mind. I feel like a cartoon character, where you can see the literal gears turning in their head when they're thinking. Creativity can also be twisted and morph into, let's say, some more unusual ideas. There was a time in my early 20s where I believed that I had found the formula for time travel. This is related to delusional thinking, but I was in such a creative zone that this is how my delusions manifested.

The problem many people find with this creativity is that when your manic stage ends, so does this creative thinking. For me, this means my life is littered with half-finished projects. Without that creative spark, I often can't find that same mindset. It's frustrating that you can't magic up this feeling. If I could bottle that creativity and the motivation to act on it, I'd sell it and make a fortune.

CONFIDENCE

Unrivalled confidence is a huge boon to the experience of hypomania and mania. Your mind feels quicker, sharper than everyone else's. The world around you feels slower and people seem to think at a snail's pace.

Picture a conversation with friends. You're out for a coffee and a chat in a local cafe. You feel the conversation is moving unbelievably slowly. It's a struggle to stay silent and listen attentively. You have things to say, and they feel much more important than what's actually being said. So you start talking and the words begin to flow. But there's more, and you start tripping over your words because you have so much to say and you're already thinking about the next two or three points you want to make. You don't care that no one else is getting a word in; your points matter and your voice is vital.

It gives you the confidence to try new things, to go for that promotion or apply for that job. It shuns indecision, and the little friend of mania on your shoulder is telling you to *go for it!* You find yourself standing up to people, becoming more assertive at work and in your personal life. Again, as with creativity, it can be a positive aspect of mania.

There is such a thing as being too confident. It can come across to others as arrogance, especially if they're unaware that you're unwell. That little friend I was talking about – well, it sometimes feeds your self-belief and inflates your ego to the point where you feel like the smartest, most alluring, talented human being on the planet. The problem with this is that everyone – and I mean everyone – seems inferior to you. They're idiotic, their opinions don't matter, and if they disagree, they're always wrong. It can alienate loved ones and colleagues, and honestly, people just think you're being a bit of a dick.

ENERGY

Having all the energy at first feels fantastic. Suddenly, there's this burst of energy that comes from nowhere. It feels as if you have this never-ending supply.

It might take the form of:

- working out excessively
- doing all the odd jobs you never quite find the time to finish
- deciding to paint every wall of your home and then still having the energy to go on a night out.

Somehow you keep going. It's as if you're running on fumes. The warning sign on the dashboard has popped up but you ignore it. The level should be too low to keep going, like a car that is sputtering and stops because it's run out of petrol. But you keep going regardless – your supply of energy feels infinite.

When I first went to university, I was manic. I wanted to experience everything. I had boundless energy in the first term. I would get up at 4am to start work at the coffee shop at the train station at 5am. After my shift, I'd go to lectures. Then back to my room to write furiously. At night, I'd go out and party. Pub, bar, nightclub. I'd roll into halls around 2 or 3am, sleep for a couple of hours and go to work. Repeat. For months, this was my routine. I've had many more experiences like this, littered across my late teens and 20s. We all have times when we feel revved up and as if we can just keep going. It might last for a couple of days and then it fades away. The difference with Bipolar is that it's sustained. It can go on for weeks and months.

> In young people, attention deficit hyperactivity disorder (ADHD) and Bipolar can be mistaken for each other, and children and teenagers may well be misdiagnosed. With Bipolar, you feel incredibly hyperactive and can't stop talking, incessantly chatting to everyone you meet. I'd go on for hours, talking about anything that came into my head.

THE NEGATIVE

Now we move on to the less fun aspects of mania and hypomania. Yes, it can definitely turn on you, without you even realizing it's a problem. It can put you in very real danger. You can end up alienating friends and family. You can find yourself in financial trouble. It's all pretty sh***y and, as I've already said, the positives of mania just don't outweigh the negatives. Manic episodes can destroy relationships and have long-lasting consequences for your life. So that's why it's so important to identify the warning signs, your triggers and the more difficult aspects of living with Bipolar, which we will explore later in this chapter.

RISK TAKING AND RECKLESS BEHAVIOUR
This symptom is by far the most dangerous. It can come in different forms and is different for everyone. It might be, for example:

- drinking and taking recreational drugs to an excessive degree
- walking home by yourself at 3am, without a phone or any money
- walking out in front of cars to cross the street and getting run over.

One experience for me has stuck in my head. When I'm manic, I'm an incredibly reckless driver. I don't mean to be, and now I don't drive when I'm having an episode of mania.

I'm at work. It's been a long shift and my mind is humming and buzzing away with ideas. The nursery I work at is in the countryside on the outskirts of Reading, off a gravel road leading to a small country road. Again, I'm bursting to escape the dull routine and find some excitement. I race to my car and tear down the gravel road, away from the nursery and the monotony of the day. My mind is impulsive, and I feel that it would be a wonderful idea to drive in the middle of the road. Delusional, I believe that everyone will move for me, that the obstructions in my way will magically disappear. It's pitch black and the windows of the car are fogged up while I'm driving.

Before I know it, there's a car driving towards me. I don't need to swerve – the car will move for me – so I speed up. I hold my breath with anticipation of what will happen next.

We collide and I scream with excitement as the car bumps and scrapes against mine. The wing mirror clips off. I squeal and laugh hysterically as I continue driving. The other car has come to a halt and I can see a figure frantically waving at me as I drive away. I'm laughing so much I'm not paying attention to the road.

I stop at a busy junction and see a gap in the traffic. It's not nearly enough of a gap for me to sensibly get through. I see a car to the side hurtling towards me, barely managing to slow down in time. I misjudge the turn and stamp on the accelerator. I don't turn the wheel enough and drive into a bollard, puncturing the driver's side front tyre. Again, I refuse to stop and continue on my way home. At the traffic lights five minutes away from home, a driver knocks at my window and shouts, 'Did you know you have a puncture?'

I wind down my window and gleefully reply, 'Yeah, I know!'

He looks at me, bewildered. 'You can't drive home like that.'

I laugh at him. My view of the world is warped and I'm delusional. I can't understand what the issue is. The fact that my car is missing a wing mirror, has a broken headlight, a massive scrape down the driver's side and now a completely flat punctured tyre doesn't indicate to me that there is a problem. So my obvious response is 'It's fine! I'm nearly home anyway!'

He stands and shakes his head as I wind the window up.

ANGER AND IRRITABILITY

When I say mania can turn, it can turn ugly.

Anger is like an iceberg. What you see on the surface can be misleading, because most of an iceberg is hidden underwater. This is how anger works. Often when we're angry, there are emotions hidden under the surface. We might be insecure, overwhelmed, stressed, feel disrespected, embarrassed, just to name a few. With Bipolar, this iceberg is intensified by the symptoms of mania or hypomania.

I have always had a temper. Except to the people closest to me, it's a side I rarely show. One of the major problems when I'm managing a manic episode is controlling my anger. I usually come across as calm and friendly, a level-headed type with a gentle nature. When I've explained I struggle with angry outbursts to people, the reaction I've had is:

'But you don't come across like that!'

'You seem like such a calm person!'

'I could never imagine you doing something like that.'

It usually begins with a general irritability, with *everything* touching a nerve. OK, everyone feels that way when they're having a bad day and we might feel as if we want to explode. With Bipolar, that irritable feeling is relentless, like a constant itch on your back you can't reach and there's no one to scratch it for you. The loudness of someone eating, the way they look at you, people getting in your way when you're walking down the street, all this is infuriating. You'll find yourself snapping at people when they don't deserve it. This might level out and you find yourself annoying and rubbing people up the wrong way for a few days or weeks. Or it might evolve into something more serious.

This anger can be very difficult to explain to others. Of all the symptoms that accompany Bipolar, the swell – well, actually the tidal wave – of anger you feel is difficult to explain and for others to grasp.

Everyone has flashes of anger. We all have those days when we just wake up in an irritable, bad mood and we can't find a reason why. We're short with everyone and snap at the smallest inconvenience or provocation. We explain it away as just a bad day, or we got out of the wrong side of the bed. We all know someone whom we describe as having a short fuse; they're a hot-head, or just a general bad-tempered grump. However, the anger associated with Bipolar is sustained and intense. It feels like a cyclical bout of anger you've trapped yourself in. You're caught in a feedback loop, and it can last for hours, ruining an evening or a whole day for you and everyone caught in it. You literally can't move past the problem. You can't calm down. Your mind won't let you, constantly going over and over it.

The anger, the real anger, is when things become serious. Sometimes it might be an explosive rant. With me, I'll shred the person to pieces with a barrage of insults, or I might angrily shout about something that happened earlier in the day. My face will become flushed; I'll grind my teeth and spit as I'm talking. I'll shout and scream until my throat is sore and my voice is hoarse. Everyone does this occasionally, but nearly always it'll be a significant argument or serious situation. It's not the same when you're in mania, with the tiniest annoyances setting you off and sparking a rant.

I've had many temper tantrums. Shouting, screaming, swearing at nothing, everyone, in people's faces, in the street and at home. I'll stamp my feet as I rant and rave. I've thrown my phone, my laptop. I've trashed my home. I've hit myself and punched walls. I had to explain to my landlord when we moved out why there was a knuckle-shaped hole in the wall. These tantrums can be a response to anything that has upset or annoyed me. Once it started because I thought a housemate had opened a package addressed to me. Another tantrum erupted because I forgot my hairbrush when I was staying at my partner's place.

Before I was diagnosed, I assumed everyone had bouts of anger similar to this but they were just better at hiding it than me. I assumed it was pre-menstrual tension, although this anger could happen at any time of the month. Deciding that this was true, in certain circumstances I began to train myself to hide how I was feeling. At work in particular, because of the nature of my previous jobs, I would nod and smile when really I was raging. I would excuse myself and go to the bathroom, where I would scream and stamp my feet. This is one of the most unhealthy coping mechanisms I've acquired over the years and is one that took me a long time to break. Returning home after work, I found that the anger would explode into viciousness and exasperation. Everyone I have lived with, or who has spent an extended period of time with me, has had to deal with this, and I've apologized many times when I've been more stable.

What can I do to manage my anger?

- Make a list of what triggers your anger – maybe it's social media or watching the news. When you've recognized what the triggers are for you, try to ignore them, if you can – for instance, staying away from social media and deleting news apps from your phone.
- Try harnessing your energy into something productive. When you can feel yourself getting upset or angry, try putting that energy into creative activities. Similarly, harness that energy through exercise, because this can help you manage your anger in a more productive way.
- Explain to loved ones that they should encourage you to do the above if you show signs of irritability or anger. Tell them you might become angry at the flip of a switch, so explain what your triggers are and the signs to watch out for. Most importantly, explain that when this happens, you're not necessarily angry at them, or attacking them, but it's just another symptom of mania.

OVERSPENDING

Finding yourself in financial trouble can be a regular occurrence after a manic episode. Often, we'll spend money frivolously. Remember that saying, 'money doesn't grow on trees'? Well, during a manic episode you act as if it does. The other problem is the belief that somehow the bills piling up will magically sort themselves out. You simply don't care. Money is irrelevant. You'll act as if you don't have a care in the world, that anything is possible.

A prime example of this was the trip to Japan that I went on a few years ago, which I mentioned earlier in the chapter. The idea occurred to me one evening and my mind became abuzz with the idea. I had to do it. There were voices in my head urging me to and I couldn't resist them. I planned to travel on my own. Years before, I had talked about going with my best friend, Vicki, but I knew she wouldn't be able to go for the foreseeable future. I booked the £600 flight and told everyone. Everyone thought it was just talk; they didn't think I would actually go through with it. I spent two weeks in Tokyo and Kyoto; I would have gone for much longer if I had managed to persuade my work to let me have more time off. I booked expensive hotel rooms, one of which was a suite on the 35th floor. I remember squealing with excitement at the floor-to-ceiling window that overlooked Shinjuku Chuo Park. There were pops of cherry blossom on the trees. Surrounding all sides were skyscrapers and, to the right, Mount Fuji could be seen in the distance.

Everything went on the credit card. I ate out at restaurants every night, I went out drinking, enjoyed trips. I bought expensive presents for my family and friends. By the time I was home, I'd racked up £4000 of debt on my credit card.

When I returned, I decided to move out and rent my own flat. I was still manic and didn't think of the consequences of this decision. I was already struggling with debt after my Japan trip. I couldn't really afford the rent, needing a guarantor to say they could help me out if I needed it, but I didn't care. Somehow I had the bravado and confidence to convince my family and the estate agent that I could afford it.

It was the coldest winter I'd ever experienced and I could barely cover the rent. I was spending between £5 and £6 a week on food. I lived off the bare essentials of bread, milk and spaghetti hoops. Many evenings I just didn't bother to eat. I would sit in a t-shirt, jumper and dressing gown under the duvet to keep warm, or listen to music and dance around the flat. I often ran out of gas for heat. The whole place was damp. When my boyfriend came over, I'd refuse his money to pay the heating bill, even though I was living in freezing temperatures.

OBSESSIONS AND IMPULSIVE BEHAVIOUR

Often with mania or hypomania, obsessions completely take over your life. It might be:

- a new project
- a hobby
- even a person.

It, or they, become your everything. It's all you can think about and talk about. People will start to notice that your focus is only on this one thing. You won't be able to concentrate on anything else, or have any other interests.

Over the years, I've become obsessed with writing a novel, starting my own business from scratch, and people. The latter has had the most negative impact on my life. When I say I was obsessed, I didn't like any of these people. In fact, I despised them. I hated them so much it was all I could think about.

I would have massive rants to anyone who would listen about how awful they were.

This is how it goes. There'll be someone in my life who annoys me. They'll frustrate me, or I'll simply decide I don't like them. My world will then revolve around this hatred. It happens, like many aspects of mania, without me noticing. To those around me, it has as much subtlety as a sledgehammer. The obsession will last for months. One of these obsessions was with a work colleague. I took an instant dislike to him. I thought he was smug and arrogant, and got his own way by talking over others. Because we worked together five days a week, I watched him and analyzed every decision he made. I disagreed with every decision, either to his face or to others. I would spend hours every week bitching to another work colleague about how unprofessional he was, or how wrong his ideas were. I would stride in front of her desk, walking this way and that as I spoke. I misconstrued every comment he made to be a jibe against me, to be combative and threatening. I became paranoid. When he'd talk to our manager, I was convinced it was about me. He had a vendetta against me and was trying to get me fired. I believed he was telling our manager that I was incompetent.

I would write reams of notes about him, about his behaviour and what I believed was wrong or unprofessional. I would present these to my manager, each time handwriting each point in my notebook, which became brimming with page upon page of my obsessive ranting. I suspected a conspiracy. The two of them had worked together before and were friends.

So my obsession and frustration turned to family and friends. It was incessant. Every night there was a new gripe. There was an unbelievably awful crime he'd committed against me, such as not answering his phone when it rang. It would be the first thing I said as I walked through the door:

'Guess what he's done this time!'

'I can't believe what he did today!'

Whoever I was talking to, they'd try to interject. I'd just steamroll over them with no ability to stop talking once I'd started. Luckily, my obsession didn't cost me my job.

THE MANIA HANGOVER

When I'm in the grips of mania, I love Bipolar. The euphoria I feel is unbelievable. The feeling is addictive and I never want it to end. The mania is unbelievably epic, as if I'm in a blockbuster movie and I'm the star. The whole universe revolves around me. Continually going through my head are thoughts that instil an enormous, gratifying confidence:

'I'm the best at everything!'

'I can do anything, be anyone!'

'Nothing can touch me, I'm invincible!'

It's a feeling like no other and yes, when it ends, I do miss it. Because, of course, like anything, it has to end.

HERE COMES THE HANGOVER...

What I hate about Bipolar, above anything else, is what I call the mania hangover. First of all, I realize I've spent far too much. Just imagine that big weekend when you're suddenly buying everyone shots, but that weekend stretches on for months. Or the clothes-and-shoes binge when you spent an evening sat in your pyjamas on the internet, but imagine it lasting for weeks.

I've found myself in crippling debt more than once, and it's cost me dearly. I feel embarrassed and a complete failure for asking for money or pleading with the bank, or phone or gas company not to cut me off.

Once the realization of my actions sets in, I start to see with clarity and I realize I've done things that I'll regret for years to come. I cheated on my ex while I was away travelling. When I was feeling stable again, the memory rushed toward me and I felt dizzy and sick over what I'd done. It was completely out of character, and I remembered it through a haze, as if I had been drunk. I can see how much stress I have put my family and friends through with my unpredictable, sometimes rage-ful emotions. I've made family and friends cry with vicious words that cut them to pieces. I've done so many embarrassing, ugly things I regret over the years that I can't fit them all into this book.

From constantly being full of energy and unable to sleep, I become emotionally and physically exhausted. I've been running on empty for weeks and not even noticed. All I want to do is to become a hermit, hide from the world in bed and eat junk food.

WHAT IT'S LIKE TO HAVE A MIXED EPISODE OF BIPOLAR

I'm sitting at a table outside a restaurant, waiting to be served. I'm with my husband who is attempting to start a conversation. The air is warm and the sun is out. Canal boats are drifting along the waterway next to where we're sitting. It should be an idyllic setting, leaving me happy and contented, but I'm not. My head is abuzz with uncontrollable thoughts. The world around me feels surreal right now. I'm seeing it through a kaleidoscope. The images keep flicking backwards and forwards, never staying still. I'm restless and on edge; my whole body feels on high alert. Everything and everyone is irritating me. The chair I'm sitting on is way too uncomfortable. My husband is talking, and right now I can't stand his voice. The laughter from the table behind us is grating on me, and I feel like screaming at them to shut up until my throat is hoarse.

My head is full of pressure; it literally hurts from all the thoughts racing in my mind. It feels as if my head is about to explode. I can feel my hands and body trembling. It feels as if I'm on the edge of a cliff with a safety net below. I know I need to jump, and if I do, there'll be a release from the ceaseless, building pressure. I can't make myself jump. It's as if my legs are stuck and I can't move forwards.

Now, suddenly, I have an overwhelming feeling of dread. It feels as if all the energy has been drained from my body and I feel utterly useless and completely broken. The pressure in my head is still there, and my mind is still racing away. The thoughts are negative and intrusive, telling me I'm worthless and pathetic and don't deserve to live. Ten minutes later, our food has arrived and I can't stop talking. My head is full of thoughts, mostly gibberish that I can't decipher. I'm laughing but I feel like crying at the same time. I don't like this feeling. I feel I'm losing my grip on who I am and the world around me. I can't concentrate because I'm trying so hard to grab hold of some type of stability.

I feel as if I'm at a crossroads, and whichever way I go, something terrible is going to happen, but I don't know what. I may be at the crossroads but some other force beyond my power is going to choose the direction I turn. Will it be mania?

Or depression? It's a terrifying feeling to seemingly have no control over your mind.

This had been going on all weekend and now it's Monday and I am mentally exhausted. We go home and I cry on the sofa, not knowing what to do with myself, as my body and mind continue to hum along with a relentless energy.

THE WARNING SIGNS

I think it's fair to say hypomania and mania are a mixed bag. On one hand, it can help you be more productive, make you feel INCREDIBLE and on top of the world. On the other hand, well, it's not so fun. The anger, recklessness and self-destructive behaviour simply cancel out any of the positives. It's simply not worth risking it. So, what can we do before, during and after an episode to help ourselves? At the top of the list is watching out for the warning signs. These are signs that should be lit up in flashing neon outside your window ten feet tall:

- **More talkative than normal?** This could be an early sign of a manic or hypomanic episode. It will involve talking endlessly about everything and anything. Your summary of the day feels to others as if you've just read aloud the entirety of *War and Peace*. You'll speak at a much faster pace than is normal for you. Words will just roll off your tongue. Further along, your mind will start rushing ahead to your next point. This can make your speech sound almost frenzied, as you might stammer, stumble over or miss out words. Even further than that, it can lead to you sometimes speaking what sounds to others like gibberish.

- **Sleeping less?** Not feeling the urge to sleep or even feeling tired is a sure sign that mania is around the corner. It can feel like a creeping compulsion to stay up later and later every night. You feel as if you can't switch off, or that you just have a case of insomnia that will pass. You might feel that there's just too much to do for you to sleep. There are ideas and projects to work on, books to read, video games to play. Sleep becomes unimportant. While your list of priorities grows, sleep falls further and further down the list. Eventually, it could escalate to the point where you stop sleeping altogether and this could go on for days or weeks.

- **Feeling unusually confident?** Yep, it may well be mania time. You might start being more opinionated than normal, and being extremely vocal about it. You'll feel more confident in your body and more attractive than you usually feel. You'll ask out that person you've felt too shy to approach. You'll say yes to opportunities and everything asked of you, because you feel as if you can handle anything right now. You'll feel as if you can do anything and no one can stop you. Other opinions begin to not even register. They don't matter. When you're right, you're 100 per cent correct. Any other opinion is entirely wrong.

- **Less control over your impulses?** What a surprise, there could be mania on the horizon. Maybe you have the impulse to suddenly quit your job and go travelling, start a new business, or you've simply had enough and want to go out and get drunk. You might start noticing that you're drinking and/or taking recreational drugs more often. Your sex drive might suddenly go through the roof.

- **Spending more money?** Your spending habits will change and you'll start buying whatever you want, whether your bank balance can take it or not. It might be buying eccentric clothes and accessories you're never going to wear; a new expensive piece of tech you've had your eye on and suddenly it feels like the perfect time to buy it. Before you know it, you'll be buying hundreds of pounds worth of LEGO® figurines at 3am (that last one might just be me). It might get to the point where you've run out of money to cover all your bills, but you don't feel worried.

- **An idea for a new project?** It could be the start of a manic or hypomanic episode. It might be painting the entire house or being more active on social media. It could be starting a creative project such as a painting or the beginnings of a novel. It could be the idea for a new business venture or organization you've had a brainwave for. If this project starts becoming an obsession and all you can think about, talk about and work on, it's more than likely the beginnings of mania.

- **Feeling reckless?** In the past, my driving has become more and reckless and dangerous. I'll think less about my own safety and not worry about the consequences of my actions.

I don't want this list to make anyone paranoid. Some of these behaviours on their own can be positive. In isolation, feeling energetic or having a surge of confidence is a sign we're in a healthy mindset. Put several or even all of these warning signs together, however, and it's a worrying glimpse of mania.

It's critical during these times to have people close to you who can spot the signs of a manic episode. Personally, I'm not always aware of changes to my behaviour and need someone to point them out. Share with them what the warning signs are for you, so they are better equipped to help you. Being made aware that your behaviour is showing signs of mania can help you stop it in its tracks. If that's not possible, it enables you to see a doctor before it becomes any worse.

My partner and family are always the first to see it. I have a glint in my eye, as many have remarked. I'm relentlessly proactive and take on far too many projects. My speech quickens, and I'm always waiting eagerly for my turn to speak, and when I do, the speech is pressured, non-stop.

I'm constantly critiquing my mood, my behaviour, for the fear of it being something more sinister. Why do I doubt my own happiness? It's a terrible thing to be continually worrying about your state of mind even when you're in a good place mentally.

TRIGGERS

Bipolar can be triggered in a number of ways and it can be different for each person. It's taken me years to correlate certain situations and experiences with the onset of a hypomanic or manic episode. Here are the triggers I've identified that affect me. Understanding your triggers for an episode of mania can help stop you from becoming manic or hypomanic. Knowing what the triggers are, you can avoid them entirely or find ways to manage them that will hopefully keep you stable for longer periods of time.

STRESS

I don't deal with stress very well, tending to bottle up unhealthily how I'm feeling and how much I'm struggling. A build-up of stress sets off an episode of mania. I'm slowly learning to recognize when I'm stressed and deal with it head-on. I'm more aware of stressful situations and plan ahead if I know an event, social situation or work will cause me stress. Looking at a stressful situation from a logical and objective point of view helps to minimize its impact. I ask myself simple, logical questions such as:

'What is the worst possible outcome?'

'How likely is that outcome?'

'What practical steps can I take to reduce the stress in this situation?'

If I find an answer to this last question, I'll ask others for help. I think this is key – knowing when to ask for help. It's too easy to keep pushing and forcing ourselves to deal with situations alone. Asking for help is not a sign of weakness. This is a notion that I still struggle with, but I am working on it.

SLEEP

If I sleep fewer than four hours a night for three or more days, I often find myself in a hypomanic or more serious manic state. During the week, I have to be strict with myself and go to bed between 10 and 11pm every night. At the weekends, I stay up later, but by Sunday again I need to turn back to my routine for bed. What I need to work on here is a more concrete bedtime routine. What usually traps me is not being able to fall asleep and then giving up and staying awake for most of the night. A routine will help me to relax and making falling asleep that much easier.

SOME TIPS FOR GETTING
A GOOD NIGHT'S SLEEP

- **Get some exercise.** Honestly, knackering yourself out can help knock you out for the night. Tiring out your body genuinely helps you sleep. It doesn't have to mean going for a run or working out at the gym. Have a dance party in the lounge, or get intimate with your partner.

- **Avoid screen time.** Screens are very bad for sleep. Stay away from TV, your phone, computer or laptop at least an hour before you go to bed. Instead, start your bedtime routine, read a book, even make a plan for the following day.

- **Try smelly stuff.** By this I mean body creams and mist sprays for your pillow. My lavender pillow is my best buddy when I'm struggling to sleep. If you don't have one, a hot water bottle works just as well, as it's comforting to have something warm and cuddly next to you – especially if you sleep alone.

- **Establish a routine.** When I was first diagnosed with Bipolar disorder, my psychologist wouldn't stop banging on about sleep hygiene. What this means is having a solid evening routine you stick to. It helps your body and mind relate certain tasks and sensory experiences to preparing for sleep. Washing your face, brushing your teeth, moisturizing your body are all a great start. Incorporate calming hobbies and interests into your routine, such as reading a book in bed or in a quiet corner of the room you sleep in.

- **Reflect and plan.** Keep a journal and write down what you've done that day. It can help you sort through your thoughts, and focus on something that might be on your mind, instead of your worries popping up when you're already in bed, trying to sleep. Writing is cathartic and can help you understand your anxieties and work through them. Listing on paper what you have to do tomorrow can stop you fixating on those plans when you're lying in bed. These tips are also great for when you're depressed and struggling to sleep.

ALCOHOL AND OTHER DRUGS

Too much alcohol and other substances have a negative impact on my mental health. They often make me depressed, and alcohol especially stops my medication working the way it should. Alcohol itself is a depressant and, teamed up with other substances I take, causes me to behave erratically for days afterwards and can lead to mania. I still drink, but not to the excesses I used to. At one point I was drinking every day, which was extremely detrimental to my mental health. People living with Bipolar are at a higher risk of developing unhealthy habits with alcohol and other drugs. This is because we often self-medicate and use substances to cope with Bipolar episodes. Often when we're manic or hypomanic, we're more likely to indulge because of a lack of impulse control. It's important to be aware of this and try to keep it in check.

TAKING ON TOO MUCH

Work, home life, socializing, unexpected events, unexpected bumps in the road – sometimes we take on far too much. Often when we feel well, we want to do *everything*. We might worry it won't last, so we say yes to all the opportunities. Then there's also just life. Commitments build up that we feel obligated to say yes to. This feeling of being overwhelmed can often be a trigger.

DRASTIC LIFE CHANGES

Anything from grief and divorce to moving house or having a

baby can trigger severe mood changes. They're often linked to the above triggers, with changes in our circumstances leading to stress, not sleeping or overusing alcohol and other drugs as a way of coping.

> If all these triggers are combined, it can be dangerous. I am much more likely to become very ill if all of these are in the mix. Stress often leads to me not being able to sleep, and in turn I will drink to help me sleep and to relax after a stressful day. Identifing these main triggers has had a positive impact for me. It's not always possible to avoid stress, but I know in these situations that I have to watch out for warning signs for a manic episode. I'll make family and friends aware that I'm stressed, and rely on their support, whether it be a listening ear or helping with the practicalities of the stressful situation.

Awareness and understanding of these triggers is empowering. I am more capable of dealing with mania or hypomania than I was a couple of years ago, and that can only lead to positive outcomes and stability.

> My psychiatrist urges the need for routine. Routine is a Bipolar sufferer's best friend. But how do you establish and stick to a routine?
>
> - **Decide what needs to be in your routine.** For example, even if you're not tired, get changed and into bed at the same time every night. Prioritize what's important to you and what tasks have to be done every day.
> - **Set small goals.** Trying to throw too much into a routine, and then not being able to do all the things you want to do, can make you feel as if you've failed. Break down what you want to achieve into smaller goals.

- **Write down your routine in a notebook or on a whiteboard.** It will act as a gentle reminder, and you can use it like a checklist. Lay out one week at a time and add to your calendar, such as an appointment or important event. Tracking your progress visually is satisfying – ticking off the last thing in your routine every night feels positive!
- **Share your routine.** Do this with someone you live with, or with someone close to you if you live alone. Sharing it will keep you accountable for following it.
- **Be consistent and follow the routine every day.** If you're exercising in the morning, for instance, stick to that. You're more likely to keep up a new routine if you follow it exactly.
- **Be prepared.** Have everything you need before starting a new routine.
- **Reward yourself with something fun.** When the routine becomes part of your day-to-day life, make sure you celebrate this.

Eventually, a routine becomes a habit. Habits are easier to stick to, because they become almost like second nature. Having a daily, general routine stops me from over-exerting myself, which is again a slippery slope towards mania.

I'm slowly getting better at managing Bipolar. It surprises me often how easy it is to slide back into old, unhealthy routines and find myself in a manic state. I'll try my hardest every time to not let that happen.

CHAPTER 4

DEPRESSION

Feeling Too Much or Nothing at All

Depression after mania is very difficult to deal with. It's such a juxtaposition and it messes with your head. When mania ends, I am empty, distraught. My energy has disappeared and I feel lost. The creativity has dissipated like fallen leaves that are turning to mulch, rotting under my feet. I feel blind and deaf. The brightness of the world that dominated my mind has gone. The voices, my internal friends, are no longer with me and I miss them. They spurred me on, encouraging my burgeoning, manic creativity.

Depression is illogical. It'll make wild accusations about you and convince you they are true. It wriggles around inside your mind, picking out your weaknesses. It distorts your thinking and leaves you feeling vulnerable and confused. It can afflict you when you're at your happiest – or, in Bipolar terms, when you're happy and stable.

Depression for me is:

- feeling everything so much it hurts

- feeling emotionally numb to the point I worry I'll never feel anything again
- suicidal thoughts
- low self-esteem.

Depression is not just about being sad, but a myriad of feelings of helplessness, guilt and hopelessness that will become progressively worse if you don't seek help. Depression is common, but still people misunderstand what it's really like to live with.

'I'm fed up.'

'I'm in such a mood at the moment.'

'I feel sorry for myself.'

These statements often lead to someone saying:

'I'm so depressed right now.'

There's a massive difference between feeling fed up and being depressed. It's not feeling sorry for yourself, or feeling a bit sad or down in the dumps. It's feeling utterly hopeless and helpless. It's feeling so desperate you may think about ending your own life. Please don't say, 'I'm depressed', when really you're just having a rough day. On the flip side, don't say, 'I'm fine', when you're crumbling inside. Please be honest and ask for help.

When I'm depressed, I'll listen to others' stories about their daily lives, but I find I don't care. There's a wall between their reality and mine. I'm a monumental nerd, with video games especially being a love of mine. Video games are interactive and have made me scream with terror and laugh with delight. But when I'm numb, I won't play. The task seems too overwhelming; the idea of being bombarded with sound and images doesn't terrify me, but seems simply like too much effort. I wouldn't be able to concentrate, and that's the way it is for everything I use for escapism.

For me, when I'm depressed, I'll stare at the wall, out of the window, at the television, not thinking or thinking too much. Not thinking is not meditative. It isn't a cathartic, self-awareness-inducing experience. It's pure nothingness. My mind is empty, devoid of emotions. Only the most basic thoughts can penetrate my mind. I don't care about anything and especially not my life, not staying alive. There's no point to anything and everything is a great effort.

I might think too much. I won't be able to escape all the thoughts circling my mind. The thoughts are negative and cruel. They tell me about all the worst aspects of myself. It's like being trapped in a room with a bully. The bully knows everything about you. Everything you've done wrong, every embarrassing thing you've ever said. They tell you there's no escape, that you'll feel this way forever. They fill you with guilt, shame and despair.

You might have heard of serotonin before, and its link to depression. So what is it? It's a chemical our bodies produce that helps regulate a ton of processes and functions around the body, including:

- appetite and digestion
- sleep
- memory
- sex drive
- our social behaviour
- our moods.

It's thought to be a neurotransmitter, or even a hormone. It's produced in the intestines, the brain and in the blood platelets in the central nervous system. With depression, we're really looking at the serotonin in our brains. It has a major impact on our moods. Serotonin can't move through the blood/brain barrier, which is why if you have low levels in your brain, your system can't make up for it using what's in your digestive system and blood. There's evidence that low levels of serotonin in the brain might contribute to depression, and this is why SSRIs are often prescribed.

With depression, my mood will sink so much I'll hardly speak to anyone. I'll begin to completely shut down and close myself off from everyone and everything. I've heard people use the analogy of feeling trapped in mud or quicksand, but I can't see, can't move. There's no will to escape, so I can't feel trapped. I'd best describe it as my own personal little universe slowly shrinking. The sparks of stars one at a time blinking out of existence. There's no grand magnificence in their end or a stricken implosion of matter; they simply disappear. It doesn't matter to me that they're missing because it's my mind quietly brushing them away.

SO WHAT IS DEPRESSION ACTUALLY LIKE?

Let's look at the different phases of depression that you can experience with Bipolar.

- Mild to moderate depression is less extreme than severe depression. It includes poor memory and having trouble concentrating, and can be accompanied by feeling panicked and anxiety problems.
- If it worsens, you're likely to feel as if everything has become difficult and you struggle to deal with everyday life. You'll be constantly waiting for when you can be alone and isolate

yourself from the outside world. Thinking will slow down and your concentration will worsen. You'll either have no appetite or you'll overeat, and either sleep will be very difficult or you'll need much more sleep than usual.

- Severe depression is much more serious. It often begins with feeling hopeless, guilty and a burden to the people around you. This can lead to thoughts of suicide. It will feel impossible to do everyday tasks.

- At its worst, you'll feel as if there is no way out, and it'll be difficult to think about anything other than ending your life. It will feel as if there will never be an end to how you're feeling, and you won't be able to look after yourself properly.

If you or someone you know is actively making plans to end their life, it's vital you find them help right away or call for an ambulance. There are useful helpline numbers at the end of this book.

THE FLOWERS IN THE VASE

Depression is cruel and devastating – it's always whispering in my ear. Embarrassed and ashamed, I will say to myself that I shouldn't feel like this, I have nothing to be depressed about. But depression doesn't work that way. I feel as if I'm brimming with shame.

It's like a vase full of water. The flowers that filled the vase have long since withered away and all that's left in the water is the debris of petals and plant life. The vase sits in the room prominently on display. Everyone who comes into the room can see it and smell it. They all know something is wrong with it; they can see no flowers inside. I will feel deeply ashamed. I'll want to hide and disappear. They all want to help and offer suggestions. It's so obvious what the answer is to them: throw the water away and add some fresh flowers. It'll brighten the room and fill it with lovely aromas. It's not as easy as that. They can't touch the vase, because the vase is mine, the room is mine and they are my guests. Everyone so desperately wants to help, but they can't. The more they want to help, the greater the shame becomes, the stronger the smell wafts throughout the room. I want to throw away the water and start afresh, but I can't. It's too heavy. I've grown used to it being there, and it has such a marked impact on my day-to-day life. There's a part of me that's clinging to it. Some part of me wants to be ashamed of the depression; it doesn't want to face that I'm ill, and the idea that I can't fix my mind alone terrifies it.

Well...that was fun, wasn't it?! That, though, is the honest truth about severe depression. It's truly all-encompassing. But don't worry; this chapter will include advice and tips on how to manage it.

'WILL I MANAGE A SHOWER TODAY?' AND OTHER GLAMOROUS QUESTIONS I ASK MYSELF WHEN DEPRESSED

The question many of us ask ourselves when we're depressed is:

'Can I summon up the energy to have a wash today?'

Honestly, having a bath or shower can feel like trying to muster up the energy and will to climb Mount Everest. You know you're grungy, you smell bad and your hair is lank, but the idea of actually doing something about it seems insurmountable. I've had times when I couldn't even face brushing my teeth.

In the mornings, you don't want to get up and face the day. In the evenings, all you want to do is collapse into bed. Teeth brushing feels like yet another task you don't have the motivation for.

It's the same with clothes. We all have a favourite comfy outfit – the one we lounge about in on a lazy Sunday when we don't have to be anywhere. It's the one we slip into after a busy day of work and snuggle up in to watch television. When you're depressed, that outfit becomes a comfort blanket. We can't imagine wearing anything else. All our other clothes feel uncomfortable. They remind us of our responsibilities. They remind us of the stresses of everyday life we just can't cope with right now.

Hygiene isn't just about our bodies, but the space we live in. I've been depressed while living alone and all I can say is wow, did I live in a mess! I lived alone in a studio flat. Even though it was a main room with an adjacent kitchen and a small shower room, I could not for the life of me keep it clean and tidy. And because, essentially, I was living in one room, the mess was *everywhere*. I was surrounded. I couldn't escape it.

It's not just that it feels like too much. You simply don't care. Why bother washing when life doesn't feel worth living? Why bother changing when you're not going anywhere? You also feel shame at your appearance. At how you've let things go. Denial can be in the mix too. Your hair isn't really that greasy. It's not that bad that you've worn the same pyjamas for a week. The mould growing in that coffee cup is now a science experiment.

The worst part – people notice. The dread you feel when you hear that knock on the door and you know it's a friend or family member. They know you're at home, because, well, you haven't exactly been out much. The shame you feel when you open the door and they see the state you're in, and the mess you're living in. I always try to accept their help, whether it's encouraging me to have a shower or even brush my hair if that's all I can manage. They might help me tidy so I can have some semblance of normality back in my life.

A FEW TIPS TO HELP YOU THROUGH A DEPRESSIVE EPISODE

- **Use dry shampoo, face wipes and mouthwash** when you feel too unwell to have a shower or bath. When you're able to have a shower or bath, make it special, so you feel as if you're having a treat.
- **Stick to your routine** (I mentioned the importance of this in the previous chapter) as much as possible. It will keep your days feeling more 'normal' and that's important if you're at home and too ill to work. Even if it's tough going, in the long run you'll feel better for it.
- **Buy some comfy clothes and pyjamas** when you're feeling well, ready for difficult times. If you have dedicated clothes that you feel comfortable in, it'll make you feel safe and secure.
- **Break tidying into manageable chunks.** Don't fixate on how messy your flat, room or house is; instead, focus on one room, even one side of a room, and tidy that. If you pick one small area to clean and tidy each day, you'll be able to keep on top of things.
- **Focus on the after.** Think about how much better you'll feel after a shower or after doing some tidying. You'll feel a sense of accomplishment and feel physically and emotionally better.
- **Accept help,** but make sure you do some of the work too, so you don't feel guilty for someone sorting everything out for you.
- **Plan some easy meals** you know you can make before you're unwell. Make sure that they don't involve much preparation or cleaning up afterwards.

SEX (OR A LACK OF IT) AND DEPRESSION

If you're in a relationship and you're depressed, the number-one issue for many couples is sex. Or, let's be honest, the absence of sex. Really, it's the absence of any intimacy.

Sex with a partner is good for us. It's good when we use protection. It's good when we know the other person is sexually healthy:

- It releases endorphins, the natural happiness chemical in our brains.
- It creates a bond with our partner.
- It's a healthy expression of our feelings for our partner.
- It's a great form of exercise!

When we're depressed, none of this matters. Sex is not on our radar. It feels like something we'll never have an interest in again. There are a few reasons why this happens. First, there's just no need for sex. Our sex drive is almost at zero, and it feels like just another task on our list of things we really don't have the motivation for. Sex drive is often linked to serotonin, which I mentioned earlier, so it could be that we're lacking this important chemical.

Something else we lose when we're depressed is our self-esteem. We'll look in the mirror and hate what we see. We don't feel attractive, and the idea that anyone could find us remotely sexy is beyond us.

When we're manic, we often feel hypersexual, and our sex drive goes through the roof. When mania ends, and we find ourselves depressed, that feeling, that compulsion, disappears. It's difficult for both sides of a relationship.

HOW DO YOU TALK TO YOUR PARTNER ABOUT SEX?

It's not an easy subject to broach, because both sides can feel insecure and that the lack of sex is their fault. It's important to talk to your partner about how Bipolar disorder affects your sex drive. If they know and are prepared for this change when you're depressed, it will be easier for them to accept. It might be awkward, but being honest that you're depressed, and that sex is just not on your radar at the moment, is so important. Making excuses for not being intimate will push your partner away. Explaining that depression is the reason will help them realize it's not them, and that it won't last forever.

If depression is making you feel uncomfortable in your skin, talk about that too. Our self-esteem can disappear when we're depressed, and intimacy is often wrapped up in how confident we feel. This isn't something that's easy to navigate and deal with, but sharing your worries and talking it through with your partner will help them understand and know they need to be supportive. Again, this lack of self-esteem will most likely not last forever, and when depression lifts, we will again feel more confident.

THE ANXIETY-DEPRESSION LINK

Depression and anxiety are often intrinsically linked. Many people with Bipolar also struggle with anxiety and panic attacks.

I had my first panic attack at 18. I was at home in bed when I was suddenly hit with a wave of nausea. I rushed downstairs to the bathroom but nothing happened. My Mum had heard me coming down the stairs and appeared at the doorway to check if I was OK. That was when the pain hit me. A sharp, intense pain penetrated my chest. It felt as if I'd been stabbed. I started to pace the house, but with each step the pain resonated from my foot up to my chest. With every action, the pain continued to intensify, as did my desperation. By that point I was crying with fear. I was convinced I was having a heart attack and I was going to die.

My Mum rushed to the phone and called an ambulance. Unable to control my breathing, I began to hyperventilate. Again, this was a new experience and I was terrified. Anyone who has experienced this knows how difficult it is to rein in your breathing pattern, especially when you don't understand what's happening to you. I didn't understand that I needed to calm myself and relax, and this would release some of the pain I was in. As my fear increased, so did the pain. It was a pain that tore through me in great swathes.

The ambulance arrived and the paramedics were incredibly calm and patient with me. At the hospital, the doctor took an ECG (electrocardiogram), which came back normal, and an X-ray of my chest and a number of blood tests; all those came back fine. The doctor's opinion was that I'd pulled a muscle in my chest, and I was sent home.

A couple of days later, my Mum floated the idea that I could have had a panic attack. I laughed at her. I thought it was ridiculous because I didn't have anything to panic about. The more I thought about it, the more I realized maybe it was true. My mood had dropped, after months of being on a high. There was this realization that I'd burnt out. My body had been screaming at me for months:

'Stop! Slow down!'

It had been telling me it had had enough. My body was going into panic mode, because I simply couldn't go on.

HAVING PANIC ATTACKS? HERE ARE A FEW TIPS TO HELP YOU THROUGH

- **Think logically.** Tell yourself, 'I know this is a panic attack. I know it's painful but it won't kill me.' When you've identified that it is a panic attack, think about how although it's painful and uncomfortable, it won't turn into anything sinister. Talk yourself through the situation by repeatedly telling yourself this. Say it with conviction, to convince yourself it will be OK.
- **Distraction.** If thinking logically doesn't work on its own, try to distract your mind. It might be watching a favourite TV show. It could be something like colouring or sketching, anything that keeps your hands busy and forces you to focus. I love video games so I might turn on the console and try to figure out that Zelda puzzle that's been bugging me. If you occupy your mind effectively and for long enough, you might not even realize that the pain and panic have gone.
- **Breathing exercises.** Try breathing through your diaphragm – it's a muscle just beneath your lungs. Sit or lie down, comfortably, and put one hand under your rib cage and one over your heart. Inhale and exhale through your nose, and you'll notice how your stomach and chest move as you breathe. Try isolating your breathing so that your stomach moves instead of your chest. There's also the option to focus on your breathing – how does it feel when you inhale and exhale? Try shutting your eyes and slowly count to four as you inhale through your nose, and exhale again, as you count to four.

DEPRESSION – IT'S NOT JUST IN YOUR HEAD

Depression can affect our whole bodies and make us feel physically ill. Your quality of life will go downhill, and that will have a dramatic effect on how you can manage emotionally and physically day to day. Depression can weaken your immune system, cause digestive problems and even lead to a higher risk of having a heart attack. There's significant proof that depression has a negative impact on our overall physical health.

Mental and physical health are inextricably linked, and when we're depressed, we often become physically ill too. It can lead to problems further down the line if we use unhealthy habits to manage depression.

A few years ago, I'd been ill with an episode of depression. I felt incredibly low, I was hardly sleeping, and I felt a crushing lack of self-worth. One day, all of a sudden, I started feeling extremely tired and dizzy. The dizziness made me feel as if I was tumbling round inside a washing machine. It was constant, whether I was lying down or standing up. It made me feel nauseous, and I couldn't concentrate. I couldn't work and just had to lie in a dark room and try to sleep. It lasted for weeks. I eventually found out it was an inner ear infection. My doctor told me they're usually caused by stress or by being rundown.

Insomnia, too, can cause illness. This happened to me when I was only managing to sleep a couple of hours every night, if I was lucky. Inevitably, I became rundown. I was desperate for sleep and I remember thinking:

'What else could go wrong?'

Well, I managed to develop an eye infection and a high fever. I felt awful and just had to lie in bed, feeling even more miserable than I already was.

The more we educate ourselves about depression, the more we can look after our general health. So it's important to understand why we become unwell in the first place. Look out for the warning signs, the early symptoms and triggers for an episode. Find a routine that works for you. Have a night-time routine to help you sleep, eat healthily and exercise regularly; sticking to this as much as you can will keep you physically well. Take time out to recharge when you spot the early symptoms of depression. Ask for help when you need it, from friends, family or your workplace.

AN OBSESSION YOU DON'T WANT

Depression is an obsession with your own self-hate. It feels like a constant train of thoughts. It makes you fixate on the worst aspects of yourself. It's as if you're lying in bed at night trying to get to sleep and you find yourself revisiting everything you've done that day. Depression does this to me constantly, except it recounts every single thing I have ever done wrong, every embarrassing situation. I'll find myself staring blankly as these thoughts intrude into my life. They scupper my plans as they paralyze me with fear and sadness. The obsession continues. The self-hate urges me to dredge up all the worst aspects of my personality and fixate on them – that I have a temper, which I take out on authority figures and family; that I can be quiet and intense, which alienates strangers and new people in my life; that I can never finish anything I start, which fuels the self-fulfilling prophecy that I'm a failure.

What can you do about this obsession? We know it's not healthy to think this way, but it's something we all do when we're depressed. How about a positivity jar? Pick up a large Mason jar and some post-it notes. When you're feeling stable and in a good frame of mind, write down, one post-it at a time, what you like about yourself. Is it your sense of humour? That you're kind and caring? Maybe you're good at making things? Add random facts about yourself that make you unique and special. Ask someone close to you what they like about you the most, and write those things down too. Add them all to the jar – and when you're feeling depressed, open the jar and read through the notes you've left yourself. It will lift your mood and remind you to love and appreciate yourself. You could go further and have a jar filled with achievements, or a jar filled with positive quotes, if that's your sort of thing.

I'M NEARING A CRISIS. WHAT CAN I DO TO HELP MYSELF?

I have what I call a 'crisis box'. OK, I know it sounds dramatic (I'll be honest, I am a bit dramatic), so you may have heard it called a 'self-care box'. It will vary from person to person, and your box will include items that are soothing and comforting for you. My 'crisis box' is all about making me feel safe and secure. It's about holding on to positive memories, and knowing that I will get through this, as I've done countless times before. Let me give you a quick tour:

- **Fluffy socks.** The feeling of softness and warmth on my feet helps ground me, and I can focus on the sensation, rather than my negative thoughts.
- **Scented candles.** For use in a nice hot bubble bath. Baths are my happy place and make me feel safe.
- **Aromatherapy rollers.** I put these on my pressure points – my wrists, behind my ears and neck. (I used to think aromatherapy was lame, but I've found it really helps to calm me down!)

- **Something to cuddle.** At the moment, it's a soft plushie, but it could be a lavender cushion or a hot water bottle. This helps, especially if you live alone, and can aid sleep.
- **A favourite movie and book.** I'll pick something that holds happy memories, that has helped me through a crisis before, or a movie or book from my childhood.
- **Helpline numbers.** I'm a scatterbrain, and even though I had numbers to ring when I was struggling, I was always losing them. Putting them all in one safe place makes it easy to access them and encourages me to use them.

When you're feeling well and stable, put together your own box; think about what has helped you in the past when you've been in a crisis, and ask someone close to you for their suggestions too.

SUICIDAL THOUGHTS

This is the big one. This is the difficult one. This is the scary one. No one wants to talk about it, but we're going to right now. Depression can become so all-encompassing that we can see no way out. That's when we start feeling suicidal. Depression can evolve into a sneering, unrelenting monster, ready to tear you to shreds. Taking your own life can feel like the only option.

I remember a time when my mood plummeted further than I could have imagined. I was done. I couldn't see a way forward. I felt totally and utterly broken. I'd been sitting at the dining-room table crying for what seemed like hours. The thoughts circling my mind were becoming too painful. I knew what I was going to do. I had a plan in place and started to put everything in order to take my own life.

Luckily for me, the phone rang. It was my Mum. She'd been checking up on me every day during the week when my partner, Jimi, was at work. She knew I was struggling but hadn't realized how on the brink I was. She heard my voice and just knew. She told me firmly, 'You need to ring the crisis team.'

I hung up and rang the number I'd been given by my psychiatrist. A woman answered with a brisk tone. I couldn't catch what she said, so I put the phone down. Often if I'm depressed, I find it difficult to keep up with a fast-paced conversation. At that moment, the voice on the end of the line was speaking far too quickly for my sluggish mind to process. Second try, same voice. This time, I managed to hear the words, 'Mental health'.

I blurted out, 'I need to talk to someone, now. I want to kill myself.'

The voice responded with, 'Ah, you must be trying to get hold of the person on duty for the crisis team today. This is the wrong number. This is the admin team; they're on another extension. I'll give you the number.'

I grabbed the nearest pen and on the back of an envelope I shakily wrote down the number. I had to ask her to repeat it several times as she rattled off the numbers. I took a deep breath and dialled again. I got through and again, through sobs and deep breaths, explained what was happening. A man with a calm, official-sounding voice asked for my name. There was a pause. The response was, 'OK, Katie, I need to go and look up your file. I will call you back.'

I had to wait 30 minutes. It wasn't just that I wanted to take my own life, I wasn't planning to – I was actively about to. You can imagine this felt like an endless, incredibly agonizing time to wait. The only thing I could see with clarity was how I was going to end everything.

There was a knock at the door. It was my Mum. She hugged

me and gripped hold of me tightly, as if this action would keep me safe from myself, and if she held on to me for long enough, it would fix me, and I'd be back to the old Katie, full of life and humour. I should have felt safer that she was there but I didn't. My mind was so preoccupied with taking my own life. I couldn't speak; I was beyond able to articulate the misery I was experiencing. We just sat at the table in silence. The phone rang and I picked it up immediately. The voice said, 'Katie, I've looked through your notes and see that you've been prescribed medication for Bipolar disorder. I suggest you continue taking the medication and you should soon start to feel better.'

Silence from both ends. I was in such a state that all I could muster was, 'OK, um, thank you.'

And that was it. I didn't have the fight to push for more help, to have someone come out to support me, to be admitted to hospital. If I'd been alone at that point, I believe I would have tried to take my own life. I wouldn't have hesitated to take those pills. I was lucky and I'm so grateful that I wasn't on my own.

I was inconsolable. I felt I'd been told there was no hope for me, that I had to keep fighting when I had no fight left. I was crying so much that I could barely breathe through the sobs. I felt devoid of life. It felt as if I was in a haze between life and death, of wanting to die and making it a reality. It didn't feel as if my mind was connected to my body any longer. The world around me felt ethereal, and it was as if I was in a trance – a trance that could only be broken by ending my life.

Mum couldn't get much sense out of me, so she sprang into action, rang my psychiatrist's office and managed to book an appointment for me the following day. I wasn't alone for the rest of the day. Jimi came home early from work to look after me. I don't remember much else from that day. The hours morphed into a muddied state of tears and an inescapable feeling of dread.

The only escape I could find was going to bed. As I lay there, I wondered if dying was like falling asleep, and how I wished that it could be that easy – that I didn't ever have to wake up from this sleep.

I know that must have been difficult to read. Suicidal feelings are never easy to talk about, but it's important to have these conversations. If you're identifying with any of this, or in the future you think you might, then make sure you know where you can access support. Have helpline and local mental health services numbers to hand (I've added some at the end of the book) and make sure close family and friends are aware of where to get help for you.

It's not always possible to stop depression in its tracks before it reaches this point. Often when we're suicidal, we're beyond what self-care techniques can do for us. We need help right now. If you feel yourself spiralling, try to talk to a medical professional as soon as you can, before it reaches this point.

WARNING SIGNS

Depression can almost feel as if it's stalking you, like a predator. It can creep up on you because the warning signs can be subtle. You might start just feeling a bit 'off' and not your normal self. Then all of a sudden it can progress unbelievably quickly and you feel as if a ton of bricks has landed on top of you. But it's also illogical and can strike us when we're at our happiest. These hard-to-spot warning signs, when put together, can give you a better idea of whether you're about to become severely depressed. They can be crucial in making sure you get help and support sooner than later.

- **Feeling tired all the time?** Being knackered after a day at work is normal, but when it's every day, whether you've been busy or not, that is a warning sign. Fatigue is one of the first signs of depression. You'll find even after a good night's sleep, you're inexplicably tired. You might feel as if you need a nap during the day and struggle to keep your eyes open. At the opposite extreme, you may experience insomnia or wake in the early hours of the morning. Tiredness can lead to forgetfulness and trouble making decisions. This can impact work and daily life. I will feel as if I'm walking around in a haze, constantly thinking about when I can finally go to bed.
- **Irritable?** Is everyone and everything touching a nerve? Well, it could be a sign of depression. You'll find you feel grumpy and constantly in a bad mood. You'll snap and lash out at people for talking to you when you're busy, getting in your way, chewing too loudly, to name a few. Something you would normally brush off or ignore now feels incredibly irritating and frustrating. People will find it hard to be around you, and you'll feel guilty about how short-tempered you've become. You'll snap at people and react to situations very differently from how you used to.
- **Lacking concentration?** It might be depression. You can be at work, trying to read a book, even trying to watch a movie, but you just can't concentrate. Focusing on something seems too big a task. You lose focus not because of distractions around you, but simply because your mind feels as if it's slowing down.
- **An increase or decrease in appetite?** Appetite changes

can spell depression. Depending on the person, our appetite changes drastically when we're depressed. You might find you have no interest in food and feel as if you're almost forcing yourself to eat. Or it might be the total opposite, and you have an insatiable hunger. Since anxiety and depression often coincide, a high level of anxiety leaves many people feeling nauseous and unable to eat. Inevitably, depression can lead to weight gain or weight loss, which can impact our self-esteem. Sometimes depression can also cause digestive problems.

- **Low self-esteem?** You'll start thinking less of yourself. You might look at your body and hate it. You'll look at something you've made or been working on and think it's awful, and want to rip up and destroy everything. At work, you might start second-guessing yourself. You'll believe your work isn't good enough, that your boss will be disappointed in your work and you might be reprimanded.

- **Socializing less?** While some of us are social butterflies, and others prefer some personal space, we all enjoy seeing friends and family to some degree. When depressed, we might feel we have nothing to say, or we can't manage being in a social situation. I enjoy going out and socializing, so it's blatantly obvious that something is wrong when I turn down an invitation, or don't show up to an event. I'll feel a knot in the pit of my stomach at the idea of socializing. You'll find yourself isolating yourself from family and friends. Without seeing friends and family, we can become isolated and lonely, which causes our mood to negatively spiral even further. The very idea of socializing can make you feel sick with worry. You'll avoid messages and phone calls and make excuses not to go out.

- **No motivation?** This isn't just an 'off' day, this is when your motivation disappears for days or weeks on end. As with a lack of concentration, having no 'get up and go' often affects your work or studies. It will feel like slogging up an endless mountain to complete a project, or go for that run, or exercise at the gym. For me, my drive and positivity can go out of the window and all I want to do is curl up on the sofa and watch TV.

- **Not enjoying your favourite hobbies or activities?** Everything in life will feel like an effort, even things you usually enjoy. I don't mean not being able to find anything good to watch on Netflix, but finding that all your passions and hobbies leave you feeling numb inside. When we're depressed, often the hobbies that once filled us with pleasure no longer have the same effect, which leaves us with an empty feeling – a common complaint of those with depression. I'm usually a creative person, but I find as depression creeps up on me, I have no impetus to paint, sketch or write. Your relationship with your partner may also change, as many people will lose their interest in sex.

If you're aware of these warning signs, it can help you prepare for an episode of depression. It's very difficult to stop it in its tracks once it's progressed to severe depression. It's important to be aware of and know your own warning signs, but, as with mania, this list isn't meant to make anyone feel constantly on edge. Having no motivation might mean you're just having a tough day or something is playing on your mind. You could be irritable because of a situation at work or in your personal life. Feeling tired could be a sign of a physical illness. On their own, each of these doesn't necessarily mean depression is on the horizon. Knowing these signs can make you feel more in control of Bipolar. Depression can't creep up on you so easily, and you can spot that predator I was talking about from further away.

Let people close to you know how you're feeling. Tell them you're worried about becoming depressed, because of the changes you've noticed in your behaviour. Ask them if they've noticed any changes in how you've been acting and if they're worried about you. Share your warning signs with your partner, close family and friends. Ask them to keep an eye out and tell you when you're acting differently.

I've become much better at spotting changes in my mood to the low side. Sometimes, however, I'll miss a change or sign that should be glaringly obvious. As I don't always realize I'm becoming depressed, I rely on my partner to keep an eye on the warning signs. Usually, though, if I do spot them, I can act or make a change before the depression becomes severe and I find myself in crisis.

If you're worried you may be depressed, make an appointment to see your doctor. Doctors' surgeries often offer longer appointments of 20 minutes rather than ten. Do ask for this. It gives you more time to explain how you're feeling and discuss options with your doctor. I always make double appointments when I'm struggling. I find it more difficult than I normally would to express how I'm feeling and to get my point of view across. An added benefit is that you won't feel rushed and pressured to explain everything before your time is up.

TRIGGERS

- **Stressful events.** Events such as a bereavement, a relationship breaking down or losing your job can all lead to depression. There's an increased risk of depression if you try to deal with your problems on your own. A big stressful event is a major trigger for those of us with Bipolar. Even something that we're looking forward to, such as a new job, graduating or moving house, can trigger an episode.

- **Personality.** You might be more vulnerable to depression if you have certain personality traits such as low self-esteem or being overly self-critical. This is where CBT can help. This is a talking therapy that looks at distorted thinking, usually about our own self-worth and the world around us.
- **Giving birth.** Women with Bipolar disorder are particularly vulnerable to depression after pregnancy. Hormonal and physical changes, and the sudden added responsibility can all lead to postnatal depression.
- **Loneliness.** We can feel alone for many reasons. Maybe someone close to us has moved away, or we've moved to a new area for college or a new job. Feeling isolated and having no one to talk to and listen to our concerns and worries can contribute to depression.
- **Alcohol and other drugs.** Trying to cope by drinking too much alcohol or taking other drugs can result in a spiral of depression, especially in teenagers. Alcohol is also a strong depressant, which makes depression worse.
- **Illness or injury.** A major illness or injury can cause us to be depressed. It's a significant event that breaks up our normal routine, disrupts our daily life and generally makes us feel sh***y.

Some of these triggers we can control, such as drinking and taking other drugs. However, it can be difficult to prepare for major life events, especially when they come out of the blue. Think back to times when you've been depressed before. Was there a significant event that contributed to it? Did something major happen just before you found yourself depressed? If you can see a pattern, then it can help you prepare for events in the future.

CHAPTER 5

PSYCHOSIS

An Unreal Reality

Psychosis isn't an easy subject to talk about. It's still seen as very taboo and it makes people uncomfortable. But people living with Bipolar do have psychosis, so I feel this is an important chapter to include. There are still many misconceptions around psychosis, and these need to be corrected. If we can break these taboos, then we'll feel more comfortable talking to people about our experiences – and that will help us feel less alone and enable us to get the support we need.

Let's break down when and who may suffer with psychosis:

- Psychosis is experienced during severe episodes of mania or depression.
- It can also occur during severe mixed-mood episodes.
- It can be a symptom of both Bipolar 1 and 2, but is more common in people with Bipolar 1.
- You won't experience psychosis if you have cyclothymia.
- You might not experience it every time you have an episode of mania or depression.

- You may experience psychosis in the future, even if you've never experienced it before.

Why am I writing about psychosis in a book about Bipolar disorder? Well, psychosis is more common in Bipolar disorder than many people think. A meta-analysis (a grouping of several studies) by Goodwin and Redfield-Jamison (2007) found that 61 per cent of people with Bipolar disorder experience at least one symptom of psychosis at some point in their lives.

You can break psychosis down into two types: hallucinations and delusions. These aren't mutually exclusive and you can either experience both at the same time or just one type.

HALLUCINATIONS

These are sensory experiences, of things that aren't actually there:

- **Auditory:** hearing voices or sounds.
- **Visual:** seeing people, objects or other phenomena.
- **Tactile:** feeling sensations on your skin, or feeling that someone is touching you.
- Other sensory experiences such as tasting or smelling something that's not really there.

DELUSIONS

These are ideas that, put simply, could not possibly be true. You'll continue to believe them, even if it makes no logical sense.

- **Paranoid delusions:** feeling threatened from some outside force, and that it may try and control, harm or kill you.
- **Delusions of grandeur:** believing you're extremely important, all-powerful or invincible.

IT'S ALL ABOUT MOODS

Psychosis in Bipolar disorder can either be mood congruent or mood incongruent. Yes, I am going to explain what that means!

Mood congruent means that the psychosis you're experiencing matches your mood. So, if you're depressed, you may have voices telling you you're worthless, or you may believe that you have some form of incurable, deadly disease. If you're manic, you may have voices encouraging you or have delusions that make you believe you're a superhero.

Mood incongruent means that the psychosis you're experiencing isn't aligned with your mood. You could, for example, have the same delusion when you're depressed or manic. This is much rarer and it's far more common for hallucinations or delusions to match your mood.

Often when we're experiencing psychosis, it can affect our thinking and speech. Racing thoughts and jumbling our words is also, as I've explained, a symptom of mania.

BIPOLAR OR SCHIZOAFFECTIVE DISORDER?

Schizoaffective disorder affects moods and thoughts, and has symptoms of Bipolar disorder and schizophrenia. The difference is that Bipolar is a mood disorder, but Schizoaffective disorder involves having hallucinations or delusions that aren't connected to mania or depression.

It's important to remember that psychosis doesn't make you dangerous or bad. Psychosis is incorrectly used as a derogatory term due to misunderstandings and prejudices. For example, I often hear people described as psychotic when they're being cruel or acting unpredictably. A friend of mine even called their ex a 'psychotic Nazi'. Politicians and public figures are constantly being described as psychotic or delusional. It's lazy and ignorant to use psychosis to negatively describe someone. Psychosis, in fact, makes you feel scared, confused, vulnerable and alone.

Those of us living with hallucinations and delusions are some of the most vulnerable in society. Feeling detached from reality and not being sure that what you're seeing or hearing is real can be terrifying. People with psychosis are far more likely to hurt themselves than others. According to the Time to Change campaign (2015), however, in the UK alone, over a third of people think those with a mental health problem could be violent. Psychosis doesn't make you a 'psycho'. It doesn't make you a 'freak'. It doesn't mean you're scary. It doesn't mean you're dangerous.

Stigma is tough to deal with, so it's important to look after yourself. Try changing your perspective – many people with these types of views don't understand psychosis and aren't intentionally trying to hurt you. For the others, well, their problem is deep-rooted in themselves and has nothing to do with you. Writing down your thoughts and feelings can help you process the prejudice you face. If this isn't for you, try something creative or make something; creating something from the pain you've experienced can help you move forward. If you can, try talking through the experience with someone you trust. I'll discuss how we can face up to and manage stigma and prejudice in more detail in Chapter 7.

BIPOLAR DEPRESSION AND HEARING VOICES

The voices I hear when I'm depressed can be terrifying. They often sound clear and concise, and feel completely separate from my own mind.

One evening, I was walking home from work on my own. I lived near a busy street, full of shops and people walking to and fro. I walked down this bustling street nearly every day and rarely felt intimidated. It was dark and the road was busy with traffic. I heard a voice from behind me. It said in a vindictive tone:

'I'm going to strap you down and rape you, bitch.'

I turned around but there was nobody there. It was horrific. I looked around again. The nearest people to me wouldn't have been audible. I carried on walking, hurriedly now, jumping out of my skin when a woman walked past me. I could feel my heart beating rapidly in my chest. I felt sick with shock and worry. I was so certain someone had threatened me. I convinced myself that someone must have been behind me. I imagined a hooded figure walking past me after the incident. I was shaking with fear as I neared home. I didn't want to be crazy. I didn't want to feel out of control, unable to do anything about what I was hearing. I didn't want my partner to think I was insane and look at me in a different light. To be afraid of me or what the voices might tell me to do. It's a horribly intrusive feeling to think your mind is actively sabotaging and scaring you.

I carried on walking with this circling my mind. When I arrived home, I told Jimi what had happened. He was adamant I rang the police, and he wouldn't let it go. I was still confused, in denial and terrified. It came down not to whether it was real, but that it felt real to me. Someone cruel and vicious had invaded my mind, as if my mind had been robbed. I felt violated, but my own mind was the culprit.

THE CAT

I sat on the sofa. I was at home alone, watching TV. I was not able to work at that time, as I was deeply depressed. The world around me felt overwhelming and I couldn't cope. I felt irritable, with everything and everyone touching a nerve. Suddenly, out of nowhere, I heard a cat. It was meowing. The meowing was loud and incessant. It felt as if it was coming from everywhere at once. But I didn't own a cat. I decided to ignore it. It had to be coming from outside the window. The neighbours often fed a local cat outside their front door, so it had to be out there crying for food. I turned the TV up and ignored the meowing. But it wouldn't stop. Ten minutes went by, then 20.

'What is wrong with this cat!'

I looked out of the window but could see no sign of a cat. I couldn't stand the noise any longer. It just wouldn't stop. It sounded distressed. In pain. It was upsetting. I felt the irritation rising inside me. I couldn't escape it. I was deeply worried that there was an animal that was hurt.

I looked out of the window again. It was pouring with rain – the type of rain that soaks you through in a second. It was not going to stop me, though. The meowing was so intrusive and inescapable that I didn't stop to put my shoes on. I wouldn't stop. I *needed* to know where this cat was. I needed to help it or make it stop for my own sanity.

I marched outside in my socks, jeans and a t-shirt. The cat wasn't in the front porch, or the neighbours' porch. I searched everywhere. The bushes outside our front window were a perfect place for a cat to hide. I got down on my hands and knees and rummaged through the bushes. It was wet and muddy and my t-shirt and jeans were soaked through already. It wasn't there.

'How can it not be here!'

I could still hear it, but couldn't make out which direction it was coming from. It was surround-sound meowing. It felt as if I had headphones on with the sound up, the meowing sounded so close.

I decided I had to look further away. I looked up and down the street. There were tons of parked cars down the road. A guy walked past me and I looked down at my feet. My pink socks were turning a greyish brown from the mud and rain. My heart sank when I realized I was going to have to check under each and every parked car.

I started walking. My feet were squelching as I hurriedly walked up the street. I walked up and down the road twice. I stopped to look under the cars, in the vain hope there would be a cat staring back at me. There were no animals to be found. I was freezing, shaking by now. My hair was sodden from the rain. This was ridiculous. What was I doing? I looked like a madwoman searching under cars with no shoes or coat on in the middle of a torrential downpour. I thought I needed to check the back garden, just in case. I checked. Nothing. Zilch. I gave up. I needed to get out of my wet clothes. I went upstairs and got changed, but the meowing followed me.

'For f**k's sake, shut up!'

What could I do to drown this out? I went back to the living room and turned the TV up once again. Two hours. Two hours of constant meowing. My irritability had risen to epic proportions. I was ready to hurl a chair through the front window. I could feel the anger rising and I didn't know what to do with it.

It stopped. As suddenly as it started, it stopped. I felt relieved, but disturbed by the experience.

WHY DID I NEED TO KNOW WHERE THE CAT WAS SO BADLY?
At the time, I hadn't spoken to anyone in my life about psychosis. The only person who knew about it was my psychiatrist. I needed this cat to be real. I didn't want to hear sounds and voices. I didn't want any of my illness to be real. I didn't want to face reality. That psychosis was a part of my life; that I heard things that no one else could.

BIPOLAR MANIA AND HEARING VOICES

I don't only hear voices when I'm depressed. I also hear them when I'm manic. Mania makes me feel euphoric, amazing, the best I've ever felt.

THE BOOK
At university, I became obsessed with writing a novel. There was a contest between the students to write 500 words a day, every day, for the first term. I took this challenge on and delved into my writing. I'd have conversations on my own, mapping out plots.

I remember instances as a teenager and young adult when I'd been in my bedroom, or at home alone, and a voice had perked up. When I'm manic, I'm already itching, ready for anything. I feel like a piece of kindling that only needs the smallest spark to set it on fire and rage – rage either with hysteria or ferocious anger. Sometimes it's the voices that provide the spark. They, or it, would start speaking to me. They who were always animated, always ready to push me further. Now, most of the conversations are a blur. They're trapped in a haze of mania. I can recall bits and pieces. All of a sudden, they could be there, and I was always happy to see them.

I'd run downstairs extremely excited, as if I'd just spoken on the phone to a friend I hadn't heard from for years. Or start running around the house, like a small child given too many sugary sweets. Full of energy, I'd wait eagerly for someone to come home so I could laugh and talk at them endlessly. I'd be desperate to share what had just happened. My family or friends would look at me, totally confused. Something would always hold me back from explaining why I was so excited. Something that knew it wasn't healthy to have such rich and fulfilling conversations with the voices in my head.

Back to university, and the book I was writing. I'm not sure how it happened, but over time a voice evolved from a character in the book. We would talk to one another. Or was the voice already there, speaking to me, and I used its personality in the book? I'm still unsure. We didn't always talk about subjects that would end up in the book; we'd talk about everything and anything. The voice had its own personality, separate to my own. It became deeply ingrained in me, and even though I never completed the book I was writing, the voice remained. To have a voice in my life that was comforting, made me laugh, helped me deal with being in a new environment, I never resented it. It instilled a confidence to meet other people, to find a boyfriend, to go out and enjoy myself.

I've never spoken about this or ever committed it to paper. It's so awkward to write about. I find it embarrassing that there's this voice, almost like a real, whole person that my mind has created.

I'M INVINCIBLE!

For years, I heard voices that were so real, so dynamic and full of energy that it felt as if they were my friends. They'd urge me on and give me a confidence boost. They made me feel that I could achieve anything. The voices would speak to me incessantly. This is the positive side of mania. The kind of mania I would happily live with. It can be an addictive state of mind. Who wouldn't want to be bursting with creative ideas and the confidence to try anything? The problem is, it never stays that way.

Psychosis, for me, morphs into something more harmful. Those smooth edges can instantly become jagged and hurt me. This sharpness takes the form of delusions. Delusional thinking is when you have a belief that can't be true. There's no evidence to support what you believe, but you're still convinced of it. A recurring belief I experience is that I can't be hurt. I truly believe I'm invincible.

Believing you're impervious to harm becomes dangerous, very quickly. In this frame of mind, I have a habit of walking out into the road without looking. The delusion I'm having has such a grip on me that I believe cars will stop for me. I'm too important to be hit; it could never possibly happen to me, because I'm protected by some invisible force. I also believe that if I'm hit (which in my mind, of course is almost impossible), I won't be hurt. I've lost count of the near misses I've had. People shouting and swearing at me to get out of the road; my partner grabbing me away from harm at the last moment. I've been knocked over twice. Somehow, both times I came away with just scrapes and bruises. This fuelled the delusions even more, as I seemingly had evidence that my beliefs were correct. I've been extremely lucky that I've never been seriously hurt.

KEEPING SECRETS AND DENIAL

I didn't tell anyone about hearing voices for years. I believed it was normal to hear voices for a long time. At least I'd convinced myself that was the case. A few years ago, for some reason I decided to look up the symptoms of psychosis. I think there was something niggling away at me that this could be a problem for me.

As I read through the list of symptoms, I began to cry. I couldn't believe this was me. It listed all of my symptoms, right there on the page, all astoundingly clear. It was so obvious. I'd been in denial. I knew then that I'd been lying to myself for years. The tears flowed because I'd known the truth years before, but I'd buried it.

I had a sudden rush of panic and fear. How could I tell anyone about this? I felt that if I told anyone about the screaming and shouting I could hear, they'd think I was disturbed and crazy. I tried a few times to reach out to people, but I could never seem to articulate how I felt or admit the problem. How do you possibly begin a conversation like that?

Finally, I decided to tell my partner, Jimi. We'd been together for five years and he'd helped me through my breakdown and all the way through diagnosis and treatment. If I could trust anyone to deal with this, it was him. I told him slowly, choosing my words carefully. He wasn't sure how to take it. The first thing he tried to do was relate to my situation. He mentioned some strange and unusual experiences he had had before. I was exasperated. I didn't want him to try to relate, because I knew he would never fully understand. I didn't need him to completely get it. I wanted to know he would still be there for me and support me through these episodes.

He was upset that I'd been struggling for so long without telling him. Not angry, just upset and worried for me. It was true that I'd been hearing disturbing sounds and threatening voices and hidden them from him. We worked through it together and, honestly, it made our relationship stronger. It also lifted me. I felt unburdened and happier for admitting to the voices.

The next people to tell were my Mum and Dad. This was a stumbling block, trying to tell my family. So I decided to write it down. Giving it to my parents to read was extremely difficult. They read through it with me sitting next to them. I could feel the stress building inside while they read, a pain shooting through my chest. They were silent for a long time. I could see the fear and anguish in their eyes. Not fear *of* me, but fear *for* me. They didn't ask questions. My Mum simply stated that they had suspected it. I was surprised. They'd never mentioned this to me, and we were and are very close. I suppose they'd been waiting for me to come to them, when I was ready. They simply accepted it.

With trepidation, I decided to publish the letter on my blog and share it on social media. There were varying reactions. Many comments were about how brave I was to share my experiences. It shouldn't be that way. To 'come out' about an illness shouldn't be brave, or met with admiration. I shouldn't need to be told I'm brave.

WHAT CAN YOU DO TO MANAGE AN EPISODE OF PSYCHOSIS?

- **Tell the people in your life.** Taking risks and reckless behaviour are signs that you might be experiencing delusional thinking. If this is happening, the people in your life need to know that you need help right now. Talk to them about the signs to watch out for, so they can be prepared to find you help.

- **Think rationally.** It's a difficult process, but you can learn to manage the hallucinations that are a part of psychosis. Remind yourself that the voices/images/ sensations can't hurt you. You're stronger than them. When you're low and the voices might be vicious and scaring you, try to rationalize it in your head. Think to yourself, yes, it's scary, but I know what it is. The experience feels very real but it can't do anything to me. Compare it to someone having a panic attack. They're not going to die. In the same way, you can tell yourself nothing bad is going to happen to you.
- **Find distractions.** If you hear voices at home, when you're alone, try to have a conversation with someone. Call a friend and ask them to talk to you. It can be about anything; it really doesn't matter. The aim is distraction. If no one is available, try something creative. Painting, drawing and writing, or using your hands to make or mend something can all help to ground you in reality and distract you from what you are hearing.
- **Ground yourself.** This simply means feeling more connected with reality. You can do this by doing practical things you enjoy. It might be gardening, cooking, crafting or making things. Using your hands to create something can make you feel more connected to the world around you.
- **Go outside.** I'm not joking. Finding green spaces like parks and gardens can make us feel more in touch with our surroundings. When you feel more in touch, you feel closer to the real world.
- **Talk back to them.** Some people find talking to a voice they hear helps them. If the voice is scaring you, telling it to go away, or that it can't hurt you, can help you

manage it. Having a conversation with the voices we hear can help us understand them.

- **Have a plan.** When you're well, create a plan of what people can do to help you when you're experiencing psychosis. This could be useful numbers to ring (included at the end of this book), what to suggest and what to say that will make you feel more in control and grounded.
- **Share your experiences.** You might find talking to other people who experience psychosis helpful. It can help you come to terms with the experience and learn useful tips to manage episodes.

WHAT ABOUT TRIGGERS AND WARNING SIGNS?

Most of the time, psychosis happens during severe mania or severe depression. It can feel as if it comes totally out of the blue during an episode. It might be because it's another symptom, like overspending in mania or feeling hopeless in depression. If you've identified your triggers for depression and mania, it's likely they'll also cover psychosis. The usual suspects of life events, stress, diet, alcohol and sleep problems are all in there as triggers. It might be that certain things make an episode of psychosis worse, so you'll want to avoid these. Sometimes, talking about psychosis can be a trigger in itself. Living with Bipolar, we all know that our brains aren't keen on helping us out, and sometimes do things that are just not helpful! If you find yourself in a situation where someone is asking you questions and you're worried about it triggering you, tell them you're not comfortable talking about it right now, or try to change the subject.

When you understand what the triggers are for you, and what makes it worse, you can make practical changes. Look at what's helped in the past and apply it. With warning signs, we're really looking at the signs of a depressive or manic episode.

WHAT KINDS OF TREATMENTS ARE THERE?

You may be offered CBT (which looks at how we process thoughts and feelings) to help you manage future episodes of psychosis.

Medications such as antipsychotics and mood stabilizers will be offered. If you've experienced psychosis for the first time, your medication might have to be adjusted.

Family therapy can help the people close to you to understand psychosis.

Art therapies help us express how we're feeling in a creative way. Whether it's through painting or other creative activities, this type of therapy is helpful if you have difficulty talking about your experiences.

CHAPTER 6

WHEN LIFE GETS IN THE WAY

Navigating Relationships, Work and Daily Life

It's impossible to live in a bubble without any stress or commitments, and avoid all the triggers that can cause a Bipolar episode. Life sometimes slaps you round the face and knocks you flat. These are the moments that can send us spiralling into depression or all the way up into hypomania or mania. There are times when we can sail through these difficult times, but sometimes we feel as if we're wading through mud and we might get stuck. So how can we deal with having a social life, a job, family, hobbies and interests *and* manage Bipolar? Well, it's not easy and sometimes we have to make adjustments – that's just reality. We also don't have to feel miserable and stressed. It's possible to find a balance and navigate life successfully.

WHAT DOES HIGH AND LOW FUNCTIONING MEAN?

- High functioning is when you live with Bipolar and you're able to work, go out socializing and generally look after yourself.

- Low functioning is the opposite. Bipolar will stop you from feeling well enough to work and look after your home and your general health.

Everyone experiences being high or low functioning at some point. If you're managing well, it's important to keep to that routine and follow those good habits. If you're struggling right now, it doesn't mean it will be that way forever.

I really don't like the definition of being 'high' or 'low' functioning. Here's why.

First, it doesn't fit with the diagnosis of Bipolar. The reality for many people living with Bipolar is that functioning changes across different days and different activities. For years, what I could manage and cope with fluctuated weekly, and sometimes even daily. Some days with Bipolar, you may be high functioning. You can go out and see friends and family. You can cook, look after yourself and do all the things on your list, or what you feel like doing that day. On days when we're low functioning, it might mean being manic or hypomanic, where we're angry and irrational, acting impulsively and a danger to ourselves. It might be being depressed and unable to get out of bed, unable to get dressed, and suicidal. At all of these times we're ill, even if we seem to be managing.

Everyone has areas of life they function better in. Some people are more academic, some creative, and others are better with people. It's the same with Bipolar. Some of us can handle having a full-time job, but our home life suffers. Others might find socializing easy, but find employment exhausting and too much to handle.

This can have an effect on how we're seen by our partners, families and peers, and even in workplaces. Many people will only see what you *can* do. If you've managed something once, then why not again? Why can't you be that way all the time? It's not realistic when you live with Bipolar. It can cause a strain on relationships and adds to the stress already related to being ill.

When you're seen as 'high functioning' in public, it can also be as tough. It often means people getting annoyed with you when you don't deliver on promises or can't give them emotional support. They don't realize all your effort is already exhausted maintaining a persona – a persona that you're coping and nothing can phase you. Commitments pile up and you can feel yourself slowly unravelling if you're not too careful. People don't understand that you're juggling Bipolar and the rest of your life all at once.

I'm what you might call high functioning, most of the time. When I'm depressed, I'll smile sweetly, laugh enthusiastically and joke with friends and family. I might go on nights out and have a good time (yes, shock, horror, you can go out and enjoy yourself with Bipolar)! I'll go to work and do my job to the best of my ability. When I'm hypomanic I somehow manage to keep it all together without turning into a whirlwind of impulsivity or anger. I've even managed to complete shifts at work when I've been hearing voices. You'd think I'd be proud of that and I am, sort of.

There are also times when I'm severely depressed or manic and this persona all comes crashing down. I'm not the only one who lives this way. Having this face of positivity and wellness all the time is exhausting and it catches up with you eventually. We don't really mean to do it. It might be resilience we've built up over the years, or we've just become experts at faking. What I know for sure is that it's not the healthiest way of coping. If you look as if you're managing fine, when really you're not, I'd say:

- **Don't be afraid to be genuine.** We need to learn to be vulnerable and to show that we're not OK. It's nothing to be ashamed of. Being genuine with someone can make your relationship stronger. Often hiding behind a mask can be exhausting. It's bound to slip, and people will get a glimpse of what's underneath. If people realize we're hiding how we really are, they could act negatively. They might be offended or disappointed that you couldn't show them the real you.
- **Don't set goals that you can't achieve.** Ask yourself, is what I want to do realistic? Will I burn out and make myself ill trying to achieve it? Am I setting myself up for disappointment if I don't reach my goal? If the answer is yes to any of these, it's simply not worth it. It's also the same for trying to do too much. What you're trying to achieve might be realistic, but if you add two, three or more goals, it can become overwhelming. Our number-one goal should always be to stay well and stable.
- **We all struggle.** Deep down, everyone struggles for one reason or another, whether they like to admit it or not. Looking constantly as if you're keeping it together isn't reality. Everyone has a persona that they keep up, to an extent. With Bipolar, we're more likely to have times when we struggle – it's just a fact. But everyone will have a time when they struggle either mentally or physically, or both.
- **It's not a sign of weakness.** Just because we're ill, it doesn't make us weak-minded. In fact, we've built up resilience and learned new ways to cope with situations. We've have to. Going through difficult periods of depression, and making it through to the other side,

shows how strong people with Bipolar are. Carrying on and living life, despite a mental illness – now that's strength personified.

WORK

Bipolar manifests itself in so many ways. Functioning varies across time, situations and people.

I had a breakdown a few years ago. I had a full-time job at the time. I worked as a family worker for a local council. This meant I ran a Children's Centre that supported vulnerable families in the local community. It was a busy job, with a range of responsibilities. I ran activities for children and their parents, postnatal groups, children's behaviour management classes and baby massage sessions, and supported parents on a one-to-one basis. I loved my job. I felt I was contributing to society and helping others.

It all came crashing down and I could no longer cope with life. I was on sick leave for six months when I decided I was too ill to return and resigned. I was later diagnosed with Bipolar disorder. Even though I had a diagnosis, I'd lost all my confidence and felt I couldn't return to a caring profession. Including the six months' sick leave, I was out of work for nearly two years. It crushed me. My work had defined me and I was immensely proud of what I did day in and day out.

I eventually felt it was time to find a job. I needed something that was calm and stress-free. A job where I could do my shift and leave without worrying about it when I got home. I found a job at an independent coffee shop and it was exactly what I needed. There was little responsibility, I had no families or children about whose welfare I worried in the middle of the night.

I worked there for just over two and a half years. I felt that it was time for a change and moved to another coffee shop. What I really wanted to do was quit coffee shop work entirely.

Even though the job wasn't as stressful, I was still struggling with Bipolar. Every other month I was finding myself too ill to work and had to take time off. I'd come to the realization that working full-time, or even reducing my hours to part-time, was too much. Being tired is a trigger for manic and depressive episodes for me. I'm stubborn and keep going even when I'm struggling, which is a trigger. When I'm ill, I need time to recuperate, and I was finding myself trying to work through it and putting that mask on at work. It was detrimental to my health and caused me to spiral further into an episode. Bipolar is a severe illness and I needed to take time to look after myself. This meant giving up work for the foreseeable future.

Five years ago, I would never have made this decision. I was too proud and work-orientated. I realize now that acting this way was only damaging my health. At the moment, I'm working as a freelance writer. This means I can pick and choose when I work and on what projects. I've already turned down work because of my health. I still struggle with not having a conventional job. There's this voice telling me I'm a failure, that I'm a pathetic loser. I try not to listen. I know I might not ever be able to hold down a 9-to-5 job, or do full-time shift work again. I'm slowly accepting this and making my peace with it. My health comes first. I want to be able to be stable for long periods and enjoy my life, and even have children at some point. This can happen now I'm focused on managing my mental health.

You don't realize until you stop working how much small talk revolves around what you do. You're at a party. You strike up a conversation with someone and the inevitable questions begin. They want to get to know you, and for some reason it begins with:

'So what do you do?'

'Where are you working at the moment?'

These are loaded questions. That feeling of dread begins to creep over you. You find yourself making excuses for not working:

'I'm in between jobs right now.'

If you can't work because of a mental illness, why should you feel ashamed? It means you're taking your health seriously and not working yourself into a crisis. There is more to life than your job. Work doesn't need to define you. If you find yourself unable to work at all, it means you've been struggling for too long. I had to give up work and I'm not ashamed any longer.

There are so many more things that define a person – their hobbies, their passions, their personality, to name a few.

I go for full honesty, every time. I say f**k their sensibilities and how talking about Bipolar might make them uncomfortable. If someone wants to get to know me, the real me, then they're going to have to understand I suffer from a mental illness. An illness that is severe enough to stop me from working. If I lie, it's only going to negatively impact on my self-esteem. I'm only hurting myself by not being truthful.

This isn't an easy approach, and I know many people find it stressful to talk about their illness for fear of being judged. If someone judges you for your illness and not working, they're not worth getting to know. They're not worth you investing your time in that friendship. The more you talk about mental illness, the easier it gets. The more people hear about these experiences, the more open and receptive they will be.

We all need money, right? We can't always get or even qualify for benefits when we're ill. So what can we do to make work that little bit easier?

- **Find your balance.** Having a work/life balance is integral to managing Bipolar. Whatever you do to relax in the evenings and at weekends, do it. Work is just that – work. It doesn't need to rule your life. We all need rest and relaxation.
- **Ask for accommodations.** If you're struggling with work, it's OK to ask for what your human resources department may call 'reasonable adjustments'. This might be flexible hours, working from home if you can, or scheduling regular catch-ups with your manager.
- **Learn to switch off.** Worrying if you locked up properly or that you should have sent that email will only stress you out. And we know that stress is a huge trigger for Bipolar. Use your commute as a way to switch gears. Listen to your favourite album or a podcast. Read a book, ring a friend. Basically, do anything that isn't work.
- **Take time off.** Don't give in to the pressure to carry on working when you're ill. It can be easy to fall into this trap when you have deadlines to meet, work on commission, or have a team that relies on you. Working through it and becoming severely ill will make any situation ten times worse, and inevitably more stressful when you go back.

EDUCATION

Bipolar can get in the way of learning and be detrimental to our studies.

If you're diagnosed at college or university, it might be best to ask if you can defer and have a break from your studies. Don't be embarrassed about deferring for a year if you need to look after yourself.

It might help to live at home while at college or university, or with trusted friends. Being away from home means you're without your support system and away from your regular routine. Studying and living away from home can be a huge upheaval, and the stress and anxiety could even bring on an episode of depression or hypomania/mania. When you throw socializing, parties and excessive drinking into the mix, it can make the risk of a mood episode even greater.

I went to university in 2004. I studied creative writing at Bath, away from my home in Reading. Because of this, I lived in halls of residence on the university campus. I was away from my routine and support net. I became very unwell, very quickly. At first it was mania, and it lasted for months. By the second term, I was burnt out and depressed.

I didn't have the energy for lectures or work, so I stopped going to both. I tried to go to the creative writing lectures but I couldn't handle the group work. Suddenly, all the confidence had been sucked out of me and there was a great void where my vivacious character once was.

I was unrecognizable in my appearance and my demeanour. I stopped wearing makeup, I didn't care if I wore the same outfit of baggy t-shirt and jeans three days in a row. I was no longer my chirpy buoyant self. It was as if I'd been replaced by a dreary, lifeless version of my former self. I would wander around the campus aimlessly on my own, trying to build up some motivation to do anything else. It was a beautiful campus, in the hills above Bath. I would walk around the lake, ignoring the picturesque surroundings, just putting one foot in front of the other, trying to waste some time before I could justify going to sleep. My head down, I'd never make eye contact with others as I roamed, as the fear was too great that I would look up and see someone I knew and have to make conversation.

Friends would knock on my door looking for me, and they would force me to go out with them. So I started sitting in the dark in my room, with the curtains closed. I would listen to music and watch TV shows on my laptop with earphones in, so no one knew I was there. I was suffering from panic attacks. I would sit in the bath for hours, trying to control my breathing and hoping the heat would somehow take the pain away. I felt completely alone.

It got to the point where I was terrified to leave my room. It was as if the world outside had become a nightmare. I was scared of everything. I knew if I stepped into that hallway, there would be an onslaught of life, life that had become cruel and chaotic to me. I would sit and not eat. There was a newsagents on campus that was a five-minute walk – a trip that would exhaust me beyond anything I'd experienced before. Being depressed in the past, I had had support from my family and I felt secure and safe in the family home. Now I felt naked and exposed, trapped in a room, safety net non-existent.

I dropped out of university at the end of the second term. I felt like a failure and I was immensely frustrated that the depression had returned.

It wasn't all doom and gloom. Later, I completed an apprenticeship in childcare and education. The support I received was incredible; I was given time off to attend therapy, regular one-to-one chats with my lecturer, and extensions on coursework when I was unwell.

Education doesn't have to be negative, and my time at university is just my own experience. With the right support in place, it's possible to have a positive experience in education. If you inform your school that you have a diagnosis of Bipolar disorder, you could be offered extra support with your studies. There are a number of proactive and practical steps you can take:

- Requesting one-to-one attention and support.
- Organizing regular meetings with your lecturers to discuss how you're coping, and what extra support you feel you might need.
- Asking for longer time limits for tests and exams, if you have problems with concentration.
- Having a note-taker in classes.
- Asking to record lectures.
- Making flash cards to help with concentration problems.

FAMILY AND FRIENDS

LET'S START WITH RELATIONSHIPS

Relationships are difficult for everyone at times, but they're even tougher when you have Bipolar. Each relationship I had before my diagnosis of Bipolar suffered. Each partner I had found it difficult to be around me. My behaviour was erratic and all over the place. A boyfriend even said to me:

> 'I don't know who you are. I never know which Katie I'm going to get.'

I didn't have a serious relationship until I was 20. I met someone on a night out and we instantly clicked. To start with, it was great. We had fun together and we both couldn't wait to see one another. We'd go out on date nights to restaurants, or go out to nightclubs and dance until the early hours of the morning. As our relationship progressed, we started to go away together, trips to the countryside. We were happy, but it didn't last. He told me he couldn't cope with my unpredictable moods any longer. When we broke up, he told me:

'I can't do this anymore. You're exhausting to be around.'

He carried on by saying he enjoyed spending time with me, but couldn't look past my bursts of anger and paranoia. And how I'd changed. I wasn't any fun to be around and it was bringing him down. He wanted an easy-going relationship. I was too intense, too high maintenance.

I quickly found myself in another relationship, after forming a bond online. It was a long-distance relationship, but we made it work. I loved her sense of humour and vibrant personality. Suddenly, though, or at least to me, she seemed exasperated over my constant chattering, my fits of rage and my lack of concentration. All of this meant I couldn't find the time to plan my trips to see her. I couldn't see there was a problem and thought she was overreacting. She told me that it was best to be just friends.

After these failed relationships, I realized that they all ended because of my behaviour. I began to see myself as flawed and broken. I felt as if I was doomed to short-term relationships, which sputtered out when they realized how difficult I was to be with.

Then I met Jimi. We met online, then started chatting over the phone. We finally decided to meet in person. We ended up having two dates in one day. We bonded over our love of all things nerdy and our similar tastes in music and literature. Our personalities were very different. We were total opposites, but it worked. He was calm and steady, and with his influence I learned to be more patient. I taught him to have more confidence in himself and to be less socially awkward. When Bipolar made things tough, instead of recoiling away, he stuck by me. And he stayed by my side through some of the most difficult times in my life. When I had a breakdown and had to leave my dream job. When I was diagnosed with Bipolar disorder. When I've been manic and unpredictable and angry, and when I've been suicidal. He's taken it all in his stride and remained compassionate and caring.

We've now been together for 11 years and it's five years since we got married. My Dad summed him up in his speech at our wedding, when he called Jimi:

'A true *gentle*man.'

What this showed me was that it *wasn't all me*. It is possible to have a healthy, long-term relationship with someone when you have Bipolar disorder. I'm proof of that. It's not easy, but never settle for someone who doesn't understand your illness. You deserve to be cared for and loved.

HOW DO YOU KEEP A RELATIONSHIP GOING?

- **Be honest.** Be honest with how you're feeling. By that I mean about Bipolar and how your relationship is going. I truly believe relationships last when you're honest with each other. If you're having a difficult time, don't hide it. If something they did when you were ill upset you, tell them. Knowing how their actions or words hurt you, and how they can rectify this or change what they do in the future, will only strengthen your partnership.

- **Stay open.** What I mean by this is checking in with
  one another. Explore your feelings and encourage your
  partner to do the same. When both sides are open,
  you know where one another stands. Encourage your
  partner to be open about how Bipolar affects them
  and how you can support each other. This also means
  being open-minded. When both sides are open to the
  fact that Bipolar can put a strain on the relationship,
  it forces you to address it and come up with remedies
  that work.
- **Talk often.** Talking, catching up with how the other is
  managing, is vital to keeping your relationship healthy.
  It's easy to get stuck in routines, doing your own thing
  and neglecting conversation. Put your phone down,
  turn the TV off and talk. Talking through even trivial
  worries is important. Not feeling heard or feeling that
  the other person doesn't have time for you can cause
  resentment. A minor gripe can become huge if you
  don't talk about it.
- **Make time for each other.** Talking regularly, having
  quality time together, is hugely important. It could be
  as small as cooking a meal together, but it shows you're
  willing to make time for that person. Being intimate, or
  even a hug every day if that's all you can manage when
  you're ill, is important.
- **Therapy.** There's no harm in seeking out therapy. There's
  specialist therapy that addresses Bipolar and can help
  your partner understand the condition better. If you
  struggle to explain the illness, this could be for you.
  If that's not your thing, couples therapy can create
  an atmosphere where you can be honest and open,
  and talk.

NOW LET'S MOVE ON TO FAMILY...

I'm lucky. I have family that have supported me with managing Bipolar. My parents have been incredible. My brothers have stuck with me.

It was actually my Mum who suggested I could have Bipolar. She mentioned it before any doctor or therapist spoke to me about the idea. At the time, she worked with young people who had behavioural problems and mental illness. She'd never encountered a child or teenager with Bipolar. However, a colleague, having heard my Mum talk about some of my behaviours, brought up Bipolar as a suggestion. At first I laughed it off, but it encouraged me to be more aware of my moods, and eventually keep a mood diary.

Even with the job my Mum had, and my Dad a qualified social worker, it still took them a long time to deal with the diagnosis. If your family have no experience of mental illness, it can feel like a monumental task to even explain what Bipolar is.

HOW DO YOU START?

You shouldn't have to 'come out' with Bipolar. Unfortunately, it can sometimes feel that way. So what can you say and how do you say it?

- **Start with the basics.** Telling family that bipolar is like having extreme mood swings might be a bit simplistic, but it's a start. If you have a description that works for you, like my faulty light switch, use it. It might be a rollercoaster, or waves in the ocean. A metaphor or description can help people wrap their heads around the idea.

    Break it down into chunks. Depression might be easier to explain, as many people have already heard of it. Explain the positive aspects of mania/hypomania, and then the negative. Really stress how these symptoms have a profound effect on you.

Give examples of past behaviour, and tell them 'this was an episode of depression', or 'that was when I was manic/hypomanic'. It will be hard work and emotional. It'll leave you feeling vulnerable, and so it's important to tell them that too.

- **Explain what it isn't.** Tell them it isn't just being a bit happy or sad. Explain you can just be happy and it not necessarily turn into hypomania/mania. It's the same with feeling low or fed up. They might say:

> 'Oh yes, I know what you mean, I've felt like that before.'

You need to explain that, no, it's not the same, but don't be dismissive. Tell them to imagine that feeling, and then double it, triple it even. It's not exaggerating to explain that you act almost as if you're drunk when manic or hypomanic. With depression, it feels as if the world is ending and there's no hope.

- **Explain your treatment.** If you've started treatment, tell them what it involves. This can alleviate their worries. You've already explained how serious it is, so they'll definitely want to know what's happening with treatment! It might be you're on medication that you take daily, or you're in therapy, or both.
- **Involve them.** Involving family helps for a few reasons. First, they'll feel calmer about you being unwell, and will feel that they're doing their bit to help you. They'll learn more about the condition. And if they feel partly responsible for you being unwell, it can help them deal with those feelings.

Take them along to see your doctor and psychiatrist. I regularly take someone from my family to appointments with me. It helps me too. Family often notice something isn't quite right with my behaviour before I realize it. If I'm very ill, having someone else in the appointment helps because you can't always process all the information you're being given. Take them to support groups or therapy sessions if you can. Share what you've learned about Bipolar and update them on how you're managing.

- **Tell them how they can help.** This is what family want to hear. If they care about you, this is all they want – to help. Make a list of what they can do practically to help you. Give them information of who to call and what to do if you become seriously ill. It can take the weight off your shoulders. You'll feel less alone knowing your family have your back. Chapter 9 is for family and friends – share it with them for practical advice and tips to help them figure out how to help you.

What I've found is that family, especially parents, are desperate to fix you. They want to stop you from feeling the way you do. They want an answer as to how you can be better again. And they want to know *why* you're ill. And the problem with these questions is that either they're messy answers or there isn't one. I had to tell my parents that they can't fix me, but they can help. My parents fretted for years that they'd done something wrong, that they'd done something that'd caused me to be this way. I've had to reassure them that it's OK, they didn't do anything wrong.

It's incredibly difficult to admit to family that something that happened to you when you were younger has contributed to you having Bipolar.

Depending on your situation, it might not be possible to be completely truthful. It could cause more harm than good. You really have to judge the situation and do what you think is best. Talk it through with a therapist, or someone you trust.

WHAT IF THEY AREN'T SUPPORTIVE?

This is tough, and it does happen. It's horrible to feel that your family don't or aren't willing to understand. It could happen for a few reasons. They might feel responsible for why you're ill, and deal with it by pushing you away. Maybe you've never really been that close. They might have old-fashioned ideas and beliefs and don't believe Bipolar is real, or think that you can 'snap out of it'.

Some of these you can work with, if you want to. If they're receptive, you can try to educate them. You might go to a support group, and you could invite them along. They might learn more about Bipolar, and see you're not the only one with the condition. You could share literature about Bipolar with them.

Unfortunately, sometimes none of this will work. It's up to you what you do with it. They might need time before they come around to the idea. Or maybe you know they will never accept it. This can be heartbreaking, and it's important to lean on other people in your life. When we feel rejected or alone, the strain can make us very ill. If you want to keep them in your life, again that's your decision. If their views are causing you pain, if the atmosphere when you're with them is toxic, then it might be time to move on.

It sounds cheesy, but you can make your own family. Friends can become your family. Real family support you, look out for you, and accept you regardless of what you're going through. You don't have to be related or brought up by them. You might not find your actual family until you're an adult. Maybe your partner's family are actually more supportive. You might be closer to your best friend's family. Tell these people the situation with your own family, and ask them for help and support when you need it. Families come in all shapes and sizes, and you can make yours look any way you want to.

SOCIAL LIFE

Having a social life and having Bipolar, it's all about balance. Personally, I need to get out and see people. I've always been sociable and love going out and seeing friends. As I've said before, socializing is an important part of managing a Bipolar diagnosis.

But it can go wrong. Often when we're manic or hypomanic, we're desperate to go out. FOMO (fear of missing out) is huge when you're in this state. Everything is heightened, and so is this feeling. We will say yes to anything and everything. Because we feel so amazing, we want to embrace it. Going out with friends is one way we feel we can do this. Then there's the charisma and confidence we exude when we're hypomanic or manic. We become the party. People want to be around us, so they invite us out. They know we'll keep going. And going. And going some more. Sounds good, but because we're ill, we can be taken advantage of. It might be people encouraging us to do more. It might be that they tell us to drink those shots, or take something when we don't even know what it is we're being offered. We might put ourselves in dangerous scenarios to impress them, or feel we're protecting them. It might take the form of sexual advances we would usually say no to. And on top of this, it will eventually wear us down and burn us out.

The flip side of this is when we're depressed and feel too ill to go anywhere. We don't want to be sociable or even feel capable of it. We often feel guilty for what we see as letting people down.

We'll get invite after invite from friends, only to turn down each one. Or we might feel we can't say no, and we turn up, hardly speak and hide in a corner the whole time. We may worry friends will lose interest in us, or get frustrated when we're depressed. We worry that they don't like us, and, actually, all they really liked was our manic behaviour.

Friends might not understand the drastic change. Going from manic/hypomanic to depressed is a huge shift. It might confuse friends who haven't seen it before. They might think you're being dramatic, awkward, attention-seeking, or just weird. They might think:

'How do you go from one weekend being the life of the party, to the next weekend refusing to answer any messages?'

How can we stop this from happening to us?

- **Let people go.** There's no point hanging on to friends who make you feel bad about yourself. No matter your connection or how long you've known them, it doesn't give them a right to use you when you're manic or make you feel guilty when you're depressed.
- **Find your tribe.** Finding like-minded people is essential. It doesn't matter if they're online or real-life friends. You can be surrounded by 'friends' but feel completely alone, because they don't understand Bipolar. Finding friends who are open-minded, compassionate and caring isn't always easy! It's worth it, though, when you finally find them, even if it's only a few close friends that you rely on. Join hobby groups, such as book clubs, walking or fitness groups and gaming nights, and get out and meet people!

- **Be honest and open about Bipolar from the beginning.**
  I don't mean just blurting it out mid-conversation,
  because that's just weird and awkward for everyone
  (believe me, I've done it). Let it happen naturally. We
  can all remember that moment when we're talking to
  a friend and we see an opportunity to mention Bipolar.
  But we bite our tongue. Later, we regret not saying
  something. Take that opportunity. With a good set of
  trusted friends, we can often admit things we could
  never admit to family.
- **Don't feel a need to 'make up' for having Bipolar.** Often
  we feel guilty for being ill. When we say no to seeing
  people, or act erratically on a night out, we feel as if
  we have to make up for it somehow. If you've done
  something inappropriate or rude, then sure, apologize.
  If you're unwell and can't go out, you don't need to
  apologize or make some grand gesture.

HOBBIES AND INTERESTS

Build into your life hobbies and interests that benefit your mental wellbeing. Find hobbies that are therapeutic; for instance,
making and creating can be calming and fulfilling. Find activities
that include other people, as this can help you make friends and
stay in touch with family.

BIG LIFE EVENTS

Bipolar and excitement don't always mix well. Bipolar and stress
especially don't mix well. Add these together and you're looking
at a full-blown manic or depressive episode, or both.

PREGNANCY AND HAVING A BABY

Having a baby can be a happy time, but it's also a big stressor. Pregnancy for someone with Bipolar disorder can be tough. There are certain medications that may cause birth defects, so some women decide to taper off their medication before or during pregnancy.

Hormonal changes can have a big impact on your moods. The risks actually grow for women after giving birth. According to the National Centre for Mental Health (2017):

- 25 per cent of women with Bipolar disorder develop postnatal depression
- after giving birth, 25 per cent of women with Bipolar disorder develop postpartum (after childbirth) psychosis.

So, your chance of becoming ill shortly after the birth of your child is around 50/50. However, if you have a mother or sister who has had a severe postpartum illness, or you have previously been ill, the chance of postpartum psychosis jumps to 50 per cent. It's important to know the risks before becoming pregnant, so you can prepare just in case you become unwell. You may have to be admitted to hospital, maybe to a mother and baby unit, so you can be admitted with your baby.

Planning a pregnancy helps you find the care you need to keep you well, or find support quickly if you're unwell. Talking to a doctor or psychiatrist before becoming pregnant means you can discuss the pros and cons, medications and what support is available in your area. Some professionals specialize in perinatal psychiatry (an interest in pregnancy and childbirth) and you may be referred to a special perinatal mental health team, or a specialist midwife.

In the real world, not every pregnancy is planned. As soon as you find out, it's really important that you find support as soon as possible. If you're on medication, *don't stop taking it.* Get advice and taper off gradually if that's what you decide. Share the risks with people in your life and prepare them for the idea that you might become poorly.

Even though it can be difficult, you *can* have children if you live with Bipolar disorder. With the right support and planning, you can be an excellent parent.

WEDDINGS

Planning a wedding has to be near the top of the list for stress, and I decided to put myself through it a few years ago. I put it on myself to have a DIY wedding. The reception was to be in a barn, and I decided to make all the decorations, the bouquet, everything. My Pinterest was brimming with images of wedding dress ideas, table decorations and general decor for the reception.

This probably sounds pretty normal for a bride-to-be. I was, however, on the brink of a full-blown manic episode, and I knew it. I gave in to it, and became utterly obsessed with finding unique objects or creating my own for the wedding. I spent a disastrous amount of money and fell into debt. I wouldn't accept help from anyone else, as I was so determined that I could do it all.

I knew this feeling of euphoria wouldn't last and, of course, as it always does, it came crashing down. I recognized I had given myself far too much to do and enlisted the help of my Mum and bridesmaids. They banded together, with my Mum generally organizing everyone! Clare made the bouquets, Vicki the boutonnieres and Hannah a shawl for me, and Hannah allowed us to use her sewing machine to make bunting. How I thought I could decorate an entire barn that could accommodate over 200 people is only known by the manic version of myself. I also gave in and asked my fiancé to do some planning.

MOVING HOUSE

Moving to a new home is undoubtedly stressful. Whether you're buying a home or renting, the process can feel long and difficult. Planning out everything you need to do when moving house helps so much. Make sure you lean on family or your partner for support, whether that's advice about the process or sharing out responsibilities.

A NEW JOB

A new job is daunting for everyone, but when you know stress can affect Bipolar disorder, it can cause us anxiety and worry. Make sure you spend time after work relaxing and taking care of yourself. Take regular breaks at work before you really need them. When we don't have Bipolar under control, we can often find ourselves hopping from one job to another. Jumping from job to job is a sign that we're unwell and need support.

STRESS

Is stress a trigger for mental illness? For me, the answer is yes. However, it's not the cause, but a trigger for an episode of mania or depression. It's usually coupled with other triggers, such as a lack of sleep, drinking alcohol or not taking medication.

I've been through many phases where stress has had an impact on my mental health. When the pressures of work have become too much, I find myself spiralling. The most likely repercussion is mania. The stress will disappear, and I'll become a whirlwind of energy and activity. Misdirected energy can lead to reckless behaviour, and I'll find myself in dangerous situations. Often I don't realize I'm stressed until I start showing signs of mania, and then at that point I don't care that stress has caused me to feel so euphoric. Of course, with Bipolar, being so hyperactive and full of relentless energy, I have to come down sooner or later. Then the stress I'm under really hits me as I fall into a depressive state.

Although stress can make us feel ill, a mental health condition has to already be there, whether it's known to you or not, to trigger a mental illness. We all go through times of stress where we feel rundown, lacking in energy and generally overwhelmed by life. If you're susceptible to depression or anxiety, the stresses of life can definitely trigger these. I find with Bipolar disorder, which I continually live with, stress exacerbates the condition. I've learned that I have to manage the stressors in my life and face up to the causes. Whether it's my job, a relationship or money worries, I need to assess the impact it is having on my stress levels, and ultimately my mental health.

Workplaces, in particular, need to work with individuals to create an environment that eases daily pressures. Society needs to be more compassionate and provide aid to those struggling for money and living in poverty. I grew up in a household where both my parents worked, yet we struggled financially. I know from first-hand experience as a child and then as an adult how much stress is caused every month when bills are overdue and you have no way of paying them.

How we effectively deal with stress can be managed through self-care techniques and adapting our work–life balance. If someone starts to show signs of mild to moderate depression or anxiety, they can seek help such as CBT or other forms of therapy for a short period. Severe mental illness, however, needs much greater intervention – a psychiatrist, hospital admissions, long-term medication and therapy. Significant lifestyle changes such as cutting out alcohol may be not advised, but desperately needed. Can you see the difference? Stress in our lives can be managed if we want to do so; mental illness cannot. Your lifestyle is a choice; mental illness is never chosen.

I think it's important here to highlight one glaringly obvious cause of stress: poverty. This can't be eradicated by a simple change in lifestyle by the individual. It's society at large that needs to work towards this. Is there a difference between the stresses of the upper and middle classes and those living in poverty? Yes, I believe there is. Are those in poverty more likely to have a severe mental illness? Again, yes. Many people with severe mental illnesses also fall into poverty because of being unable to work. This exacerbates already difficult-to-manage conditions and leaves the individual extremely vulnerable to self-medicating, self-harm and suicide.

It doesn't make you weak or less resilient because stress triggers your mental illness. Living with Bipolar *and* getting through stressful life events shows just how strong you really are. In times of extreme stress, those with mental illnesses suffer; it's unavoidable. What is important is how you manage it and getting through to the other side.

CHAPTER 7

SOME PEOPLE JUST DON'T GET IT

Facing Stigma and Discrimination

So, what are stigma and discrimination? Let's start with stigma.

Stigma is when someone holds a negative view or misconception of something or someone. It's believing, for instance, 'everyone with a mental illness is lazy'. It causes that group of people to feel devalued and that others think less of them. Someone who holds stigmatizing views may go on to discriminate against that group of people. It's not the same as discrimination.

Discrimination includes different and unfair treatment, but there are different types and meanings. Ultimately, discrimination is being treated unfairly because of your mental illness.

- Direct discrimination is when you're unfairly treated directly. It might be you're not offered a job because you have Bipolar disorder.
- Indirect discrimination is when there's a policy or rule that applies to everyone, but has a worse effect on you because of your Bipolar.
- You could be discriminated against because of something that

happens because of Bipolar. It might be that you're given a disciplinary warning at work because of being off sick due to Bipolar.

- Harassment is behaviour that's unwanted and you find offensive. It might make you feel intimidated or humiliated. It could be through written words or spoken abuse.
- Victimization is when someone treats you badly because you complain about discrimination.
- Someone might be asked to make reasonable adjustments, for instance, to help you at work, but refuses to make the changes.

Unfortunately, though, we're all going to encounter people who *just don't get it*. Some people haven't caught up yet; some refuse to listen or to change their views. They're dug in and they never want to change. It might be that they've been brought up to think a certain way, or they've had a bad experience. Either way, it's up to people like you and me to challenge their misconceptions. We shouldn't be alone, though; mental health charities, governments and the media should all be on our side. But that's in an ideal world, and we know life doesn't always work that way. I'll share my own experiences of stigma and discrimination, but this chapter won't all be doom and gloom. I'll also share how I cope with stigma and what we can do to protect ourselves from discrimination.

MEDICATION

Every evening at 10pm, my husband's phone starts to beep. It's a daily alarm to remind me to take my medication. I go to the kitchen drawer where the tablets are kept and, rustling around (because it's our shove-everything-we-don't-know-where-to-put drawer), I'll find them. I'll take 100mg Lamotrigine, 50mg Aripiprazole and 50mg Sertraline. They're a combination of a mood stabilizer, an antipsychotic and an antidepressant. Taking medication is a part of my night-time routine, the same as washing my face and brushing my teeth. I never hesitate to put them in my mouth and swallow them with a gulp of water.

These tiny pills keep me stable. They allow me to function and get up in the morning. They counter the negative thoughts that lead me to feeling desperately depressed and suicidal. They stop any manic episode from emerging and causing me to become a whirlwind of self-destructive hyperactivity. They silence the cruel and vicious voices in my head when I'm depressed, or the delusions that make me believe I can do anything when I'm manic. With all that in mind, why would I not take them? Why would I choose to be poorly? I've learned that I can't live without medication; otherwise, Bipolar completely overruns my life. It sweeps in like a high tide, submerging my true self, and the low tide never arrives. It controls my life, and I'm resolute that I'll never knowingly let that happen again.

It's possible that you might encounter stigma that you take medication. It's not a weakness or a flaw in my character to take medication. I'm not naive; I haven't blindly allowed a doctor to prescribe them. It took a long time to come to terms with the fact that I needed medication to survive. Long discussions with my psychiatrist allowed me to make informed decisions about what approach I wanted to pursue with my treatment. I didn't settle for meds that left me with debilitating side effects. I tried a number of meds and combinations of them to find what worked for me. It was a long process but ultimately more than worth the time and effort.

I've always subscribed to the idea that those living with

long-term mental illnesses are strong. We manage to live through our struggles every day and emerge stronger than we were, whether we realize it or not. Part of our strength comes from admitting we need help. It takes someone of a firm and resolute character to come to the realization that their poor mental health is having a marked effect on their life. To take medication when there is still shame and stigma surrounding it proves we can withstand the negativity.

Of course, the choice is there for us. I fully support and understand when someone doesn't want to take medication. Therapy and lifestyle changes are enough for some. What I disagree with is being shamed or being seen as not as strong as these individuals. I am. We are. Every evening when I take those tablets, I'm not seeing them as a sign of weakness. I haven't failed. With them, I've achieved so much and become a healthier version of myself.

I'M NOT DANGEROUS

I fell into a low mood one August. I knew I was in a bad place when one morning there was a knock on my door. I got up, bleary-eyed, and opened it. It was my manager who'd turned up at my flat because I wasn't answering my phone. She told me it was 9.30 in the morning and I should have been at work at 8. She'd been worried that something had happened to me because I lived alone. When I'd woken up properly, I became a sobbing mess. I got dressed and followed her into work. I arrived, with red puffy eyes from crying. Everyone watched me walk in through the large wraparound windows. I was told it would be too dangerous for the children if I worked that day. I look back at this statement now:

'You would be a danger to the children in your care.'

And you know what? It fills me with rage. At the time, I was so ill I couldn't see through the thinly veiled discrimination aimed at me. I was depressed, not dangerous. This assumption that I couldn't do my job was much more harmful to me than anything that would have happened while I looked after the children. Depression doesn't make a person negligent, and I always worked to the best of my abilities. Maybe I needed a couple of days off. But it should have been a different conversation. We should have discussed how a break would be best for me, rather than them telling me I was a danger because I was crying. That statement made me feel as if I was broken, sh*t at my job, and that mental illness had turned me into a monster. It was a monster that continued to morph and evolve, and I felt completely lost to it. What was worse was that it felt as if the people around me were recognizing this creature, and their reactions were ones of fear and repulsion. I'm sure the reaction I received pushed my mood deeper into depression.

YES, I'M DEPRESSED...BUT I'M NOT CONSTANTLY MISERABLE

It's safe to say I've gone through some difficult times and been severely depressed. I've really struggled…

I've been out to gigs and partied with friends. I've had days when I've laughed, joked and messed around. I've been out to restaurants with my partner, and had coffee dates with friends.

You see, depression is complicated. It isn't just staring into space, lying in bed or on the sofa in your pyjamas. You can laugh and cry uncontrollably in the same week. However, people expect you to:

- spend all day, every day sitting crouched in a corner, clutching your head
- not get out of bed
- draw the curtains and not turn any lights on
- never even think about going outside
- look sad and despondent at all times
- not smile
- always wear black
- not post on social media, unless it's about how depressed you are.

We're all different, and how depression manifests itself is different for each of us. There are ups and downs within a depressive episode. This is what many people don't understand and find it difficult to wrap their heads around.

It's not just that people expect certain behaviour from you; they're almost insulted when you don't act that way. We've all had people say to us:

'But I thought you were ill?'

'You must be better now, right?!'

You can almost see the disapproval on their faces when you say you're still ill and struggling. Because of reactions like this, I would not always tell people that I was ill. Or I would lie about what I did at the weekend. I would think they'd assume I was faking, that they might even take it to the boss and I'd be given a disciplinary warning from work. So I would isolate myself and sit at home.

> But you know what? We're allowed to have a good time. We can still have a social life even when we're having a bad time during an episode of depression. I understand it's difficult for people. When you haven't experienced something, it's tough to empathize. All we expect from people is to try – to listen and put themselves in our shoes.
>
> What I want to spell out is that *you can have Bipolar and have a social life.* When you have that inkling of stability, embrace it. That party you were invited to a couple of weeks ago, that you were thinking of turning down? Go to it. Don't think twice about not going. Socializing is an important part of maintaining a healthy mind, so I see it as part of managing Bipolar.

If you have Bipolar, or any mental illness really, and you're seen enjoying yourself, you're a fraud. You're faking it. Don't believe any of this stigmatizing bullsh*t. Only you know your own limits and how you're managing.

FEELING LIKE A 'FAKER'

Often I look perfectly well. I get out of bed every morning, have a shower and put on clean clothes. I might apply some makeup if I feel like it. I'll smile and chat and have a laugh.

But I'm not OK. I'm as far away from OK as you can get. I'll feel as if I'm on the edge of a precipice, and barely clinging on. Having Bipolar means understanding what it's like to have an invisible illness.

Then it's all change, and I'll have a good day, good weeks and, if I'm lucky, some good months. These are the times I can get on with life. I can do things and enjoy living without the ogre of Bipolar looming large. There's a voice, though, inside my head. A voice so many of us with Bipolar have, that can consume our thoughts:

'There's nothing wrong with you. You're faking it.'

'You're just lazy.'

'You're only acting this way for attention.'

'You're making it all up.'

I know that so many of us are living with this internal voice telling us we're faking it. For me, it comes from years of misdiagnosis. It's the worry that maybe this diagnosis is wrong too, and actually, really, there was never anything wrong. Even after nearly a decade of being diagnosed with Bipolar 1, I still compare myself to others with the condition. I'll have moments when I'll convince myself I'm fine. Deep down, though, I know Bipolar is a complex disorder and everyone has a different experience of it.

So where does it come from?

It often comes from people misunderstanding mental illnesses, believing sensationalist ideas or having broad, generalized views like:

'I don't believe in mental illness.'

'Medication and psychiatry is all a lie.'

When you're told everything that's happening in your mind,

feelings that are so intense, is actually fake and a lie, it's suffocating. Because Bipolar is invisible, it's difficult for people to relate to us or understand. People want an explanation for behaviour, and because they can't see it, they look for other ways of defining what it means.

> As humans, we want answers. We want to fix what is broken. There aren't any quick fixes. For some of us, it's a lifetime of mending over and over again what's broken. I know that seeing a psychiatrist and taking medication have saved my life. I know that I wouldn't be here without the intervention of medication and lifestyle changes. No amount of calming baths and cups of tea can have the same effect. I have to remind myself of this. I know I need to educate and inform family, friends and even strangers about Bipolar. The more people I talk to, the quieter that voice becomes.

SO IS THIS WHY WE'RE ALWAYS APOLOGIZING?

'Sorry.'

'Sorry I let you down.'

'Sorry I couldn't make it.'

'Sorry for having Bipolar and being ill.'

For many of us with Bipolar, I think it's so ingrained to apologize that we do it without really noticing. We find ourselves saying it before we've realized what we've said, and what it implies. Apologizing implies it's our fault. Bipolar is not your fault. You didn't cause yourself to be ill and you certainly didn't ask for it.

WHY DO WE DO IT, THEN?

- Mental illnesses are often seen as a sign of weakness. You have the *Just snap out of it'* team and the *'Cheer up'* brigade. We're told by both we need to be more resilient. If we were mentally stronger, we could just get on with life.
- It's seen as a character flaw. There's something wrong with how we think, how we live, that can easily be fixed. We're just being lazy, so exercising regularly and working hard will cure us.
- Guilt. We can find ourselves feeling guilty for a multitude of reasons. Our room or home is a mess. We can't get out of bed. We cancel plans with family and friends.

The key to all of this is to surround yourself with accepting individuals. Keep hold of those friends who understand, the ones who really mean it when they tell you it's OK. Those who make you feel less, who make you feel guilty – cut them out of your life if you have to. Educate the rest. We need to show ourselves some compassion. We need to truly believe that we're not at fault for being ill. We shouldn't have to apologize for it, even if some people think we should. We may not always realize it, but to go through what we do every day, we are incredibly strong.

PLEASE DON'T SAY IT...

'Cheer up!'

I've heard these and all the variants:

'Snap out of it!'

'Look on the bright side!'

'People have it worse than you.'

'What have you got to be upset about?'

Either people don't know what to say to you so they repeat these clichés, or they're frustrated that you are ill and they don't know how to help. Sometimes people are just ignorant.

'I'm a bit Bipolar sometimes.'

Mood swings are not the same as experiencing Bipolar episodes. Mania, hypomania and severe depression are self-destructive and debilitating. Mania and depression can last for weeks or months, or cycle rapidly from one to another.

'Are you a creative genius?'

I definitely believe this when I'm manic! Really, though, we're just like everyone else. We don't have a predisposition to be creative. We all have strengths and weaknesses, like everyone else.

'Are you sure you have Bipolar?'

I am very, *very* sure. It took over a decade for me to be diagnosed. Bipolar has caused massive upheavals in my life. When someone asks this question, it's down to a lack of information and education. Before my diagnosis, I never thought it would be me with Bipolar. It never even registered it could be a possibility.

'You don't seem as if you have Bipolar.'

Do they think we should be running around screaming and shouting and being 'wacky' and 'crazy'? Or huddled in the corner clutching our head, swaying backwards and forwards? Bipolar isn't the definition of who we are as people.

'Is this the Bipolar talking?'

I have my own thoughts, feelings and personality that aren't controlled by Bipolar. Everyone has mood swings to a degree; everyone has good days and bad days. It's extremely difficult when people are constantly second-guessing or trying to interpret what you're saying or how you're acting.

'Have you tried to commit suicide?'

Suicide isn't a crime, so using the word 'commit' is wrong. But really, why would you ask someone this? If you're already depressed, this can be very triggering and make you further spiral down. It triggers ideas, plans and previous thoughts.

'Do you really need to take all that medication?'

Yes, yes, I do.

'You can't have Bipolar, you seem so nice!'

Bipolar isn't a character flaw. I've found that people I've met with Bipolar have a huge amount of empathy for others. They're often willing to support others even when they themselves are struggling.

If someone says one of the above to you, or anything inappropriate about Bipolar, call them out, if you can. If you don't, they'll just keep repeating it, and won't realize that what they said was hurtful or insulting. If we bottle up how we feel, it can cause resentment to build up. We'll feel worse in the long run, which will only further impact our mental health. Talk it out calmly, there and then. You could try writing down how you feel, if you find it difficult to talk about what they said that upset you.

WE'RE SHARING - NOT ATTENTION-SEEKING

I talk about Bipolar a lot. I'm not ashamed of that. Unfortunately, being so honest leaves me open to criticism. Mostly, that I'm attention-seeking. Why is talking met with such ferocious negativity? People think we're exaggerating what we go through for a reaction. Some people assume we must be 'cured' by now and somehow by talking about it we're damaging our chances of recovering. In reality, some of us are just trying to learn to manage Bipolar. I've caught myself thinking:

'Should I really be saying this?'

Or:

'No one really needs to hear this.'

This all ties in with believing we're a burden to our friends and family. It's people accusing me of attention-seeking that make me feel this way. Instead of helping, it causes many of us to shut ourselves off and isolate from the people who could help.

Everyone needs attention, right? No one likes to feel ignored or that their opinions don't matter. We all have our own unique perspective on life. We all have our own story to share. The world needs more stories – stories that are real and full of raw emotion. Opening up makes us feel vulnerable and exposed. It's a difficult and uncomfortable feeling to sit with. Anyone who talks publicly about Bipolar has been through a long process of confusion, self-doubt and fear. To then label them as self-serving and just wanting attention and sympathy is insulting. You might as well tell that person that their journey is meaningless. I *want* to hear about their journey and cheer them on for taking that leap.

Talking, at its core, is good for us. Talking, even if it's only to family and friends, can still help. Opening up and being honest about what we're struggling with means we're allowing people who care about us to figure out how they can offer support.

The idea that talking about mental illness is attention-seeking is a result of stigma. Explaining and describing how you're feeling and how it impacts your life can help reduce the stigma we face. What many of us want is acceptance. We want people to have a better understanding of what we live with.

Making people more aware of mental illness can only be a good thing. Raising the profile of mental illness leads to more people in the general public realizing it isn't an isolated problem. If they know about the long waiting times for support, the stories of very poorly people being let down while in hospital or under the care of a mental health team, it might result in change.

HOW TO MANAGE STIGMA – AND EDUCATE OTHERS

Facing stigma is painful. It hurts us, and we need to make people aware of this. For instance, family members shouldn't be given a free pass when they make stigmatizing comments about Bipolar.

There's always one, isn't there? Sometimes there are two or more. I'm talking about family and that person who makes inappropriate statements. It can be super awkward when you live with a mental illness and that individual starts saying something wildly out of line.

I'm used to stigmatizing comments, but it feels different when it's coming from family. It feels more hurtful, more destructive to my self-worth. This is a person who should accept me unconditionally, and part of that is learning and educating themselves about mental illness. When they don't make the effort to understand, they're diminishing the battle I've been through.

We often make exceptions for family, such as 'it's a generational thing' or 'they're just having a laugh', instead of confronting them on their ignorance. We don't want to make a scene at a family party and be seen as the one that ruins the day. There's this habitual behaviour in many families of keeping quiet and not being honest in order to retain the status quo. It doesn't help anyone and just fuels resentment.

It's far healthier to start a conversation with that family member and tell them how it made you feel. They may disagree, they may react negatively, but staying silent and excusing their comments doesn't help anyone. If they truly care about you, they will reflect on what they've said and how it impacts you and others.

Next time, tell them how their words made you feel. I don't believe in letting things linger. I hope it will help them see that flippant remarks can be deeply hurtful.

Some people, unfortunately, will never get it. Their views are so embedded they can't see any other way. Arm yourself with statistics, phrases and knowledge about Bipolar that you can pull out when you need to. An example was when I was at a party and started speaking to a group I didn't know very well. We got on to the subject of one of their friends, who was being accused of faking Bipolar. They felt she was attention-seeking and were scathing about her. Then came the inevitable comment about the status of Bipolar in society right now. One girl chimed in and had this to say:

'Well, everyone these days has Bipolar, because it's "in" and fashionable.'

There were nods of agreement. The very idea makes my blood boil. I decided it was time to speak up and educate them. I said:

'I have Bipolar. It took 12 years for me to be diagnosed. It's not fashionable – in fact, it's terrifying and debilitating.'

I went on to tell them about the blog I wrote about Bipolar and to recommend some websites and books that they should take a look at. There's still a long way to go in educating people about Bipolar. People are quick to judge and repeat stigmatizing myths they've heard. But you can do it.

To me, Bipolar will never be fashionable. It's a lifelong and severe mental illness that takes determination to live with and even more work and drive to find stability. People seem to hold on to the idea that Bipolar can make you more interesting, that others will see you as edgy and vibrant, or brooding and mysterious. But this is harmful to those who are suffering and trying to reach or maintain stability.

We're not always comfortable with calling people out. Sometimes it's not possible, or we feel too anxious about it. That's OK.

So how can you educate others about Bipolar without it feeling like confrontation?

- **Blogging.** It can be a powerful tool to educate and inform people about the realities of Bipolar. You can stay anonymous if you're not comfortable with strangers knowing your name, or you're worried about family or your work stumbling across your blog. You can explain what stigma and discrimination you've faced, how it's affected you, and what Bipolar is really like to live with. Blogging on most sites is also free with a basic package, and these sites are simple to set up and maintain.
- **Write an open letter.** Writing a letter can help you explain why what someone has said to you has hurt and upset you. It could include information and facts about Bipolar that they might not be aware of. Make the letter about you, not about their words or actions. If you explain how you feel, it won't feel like confrontation.

Taking care of your mental wellbeing is the best antidote to prejudice and stigma. Showing your strength and determination (whether that's just getting through each day, or your personal achievements) in spite of Bipolar proves people wrong.

How can you take care of yourself when you're facing stigma?

- **Writing a journal.** This can be in a notebook, on a computer or even just on slips of paper! It's a helpful habit to get into, and especially helps when you feel uncertain, isolated or are going through a stressful period – all of which can happen when you're dealing with stigma or discrimination. If you're dealing with stigma, putting it all down on paper helps you process your emotions and feelings. You might get to the bottom of why you feel the way you do – and what you can do about it. If you can't do anything about it, it acts like a release. Writing it down, just getting those thoughts out of your head and reading them to yourself, is really beneficial. You might just want to rip up the notes you've made and throw them away – it's a cathartic experience. You can feel as if those thoughts and experiences no longer have control over you.

- **Talking it through.** Similar to writing a journal, talking it through with a trusted loved one can ease the stress and anxiety you might feel. The person you're talking to may have experienced a form of stigma in their life, and may be able to give you advice and understand what you're going through. If you feel that you can't share with anyone, try making a video journal instead. Like writing it down, speaking out loud about the experience can feel like a release. Expressing how you feel is much healthier than bottling up your emotions. Talking it through might be the best option if you're not comfortable writing and articulating your thoughts out loud comes more naturally to you.

- **Focusing on your strengths.** Often when living with Bipolar, it's easy to feel that it's the main thing people see about us. This is especially so when we're facing stigma and we're being bombarded by negative opinions. Instead of fixating on what people are saying about you, focus on your strengths. What are you good at? What do you like about your personality? What makes you unique? Delve into the positivity jar I was talking about in Chapter 4 to remind yourself what you and others like about you.

WHAT CAN YOU DO TO PROTECT YOURSELF FROM DISCRIMINATION?

DEPENDING ON WHERE YOU LIVE, YOUR RIGHTS COULD DIFFER

In the UK, the one to remember is the Equality Act 2010. It protects anyone with a disability, including those with mental illness, from discrimination. You'll have to show that Bipolar is a disability. It'll protect you when you are:

- in the workplace, if you're made redundant or are sacked, and even if you're applying for a job. When you apply for a job and go for an interview, you don't have to disclose that you have Bipolar disorder, and they can't ask you questions about it. If you can't sort out or challenge the discrimination informally, you can make a claim to an Employment Tribunal. You could be offered financial compensation if it agrees you've been discriminated against.
- buying or renting a property. When you're renting a property, you can ask for what's called reasonable adjustments. This might be redirecting your mail about rent and other tenancy issues to a family member or friend, for instance. If you've been discriminated against, first it's best to raise the issue informally, then follow what they should have as a formal complaints procedure. If that doesn't work, you can make a legal claim, through a county court.
- using services such as shops and insurance companies
- using public services such as the police or claiming benefits.

In the US, it's all about the Americans with Disabilities Act (ADA). Again, it's a civil rights law that was put in place in 1990 to stop discrimination for those with disabilities, including mental illness. Its aim is to make sure those with disabilities have the same rights and opportunities as everyone else. It will protect you in:

- the workplace, where employers have to make reasonable accommodations for applicants and employees. You don't have to disclose your illness when applying or interviewing for a job. If you're asked to have a medical exam before starting a job, your job offer can only be withdrawn if you can't fulfil the role, even with reasonable adjustments.
- state and local government services
- public accommodation and in commercial facilities.

CHAPTER 8

STAYING STABLE AND LIKING IT

Stability is always the aim if you live with Bipolar. How can you reach it and how do you maintain it? I'll try to answer these questions throughout this chapter. Often stability is about being proactive and making positive changes.

RECOVERY VS MANAGEMENT

The word 'recovery' means very different things to different people and it can be problematic. For people who feel they can't recover, the word can be ultimately damaging. When people talk about recovery, it marginalizes those who can't recover.

Some people use the word 'recovery' to describe a process and not an actual milestone. Some might see it as having a positive outlook, which they see as a form of recovery. Others actually use it to mean being in a stable place and free from mental illness. 'Clinical recovery' is a term many mental health professionals use to describe someone who no longer presents symptoms of Bipolar.

152

I PREFER TO SAY MANAGE RATHER THAN RECOVER

Managing to me signals acceptance, that the person has come to the point where they're no longer in denial. They're now willing to find a way to manage the condition they're faced with. This isn't a phenomenon categorized just for Bipolar and mental illness, but for many physical health problems. Managing diabetes and other long-term illnesses comes with similar challenges.

ULTIMATELY, IT'S ABOUT BUILDING SOMETHING NEW FOR MYSELF

I can't go back to who I was before. I don't recognize that person. For a start, she was a young teenager. Without mental illness and its impact, I would be an entirely different person. Would I even want to be that person? I have no idea.

If you're not seen as moving forward, you end up feeling like a failure. There's so much pressure to be better, to be able to work and socialize, to be a productive member of society. The impetus is put on recovery above helping those for whom it isn't feasible. It's this unattainable goal that's set for us that so many with severe and enduring mental illness fail at. Why isn't there more support for those who need and want to manage Bipolar? There's this idea that we can recover if only we try hard enough. For some of us, it's an impossibly high standard to measure up to.

I'm not here to be an inspiration. I'm not someone who is going to miraculously be better and totally stable for the rest of my life. It's not realistic. I can't pretend that everything is going to be OK. I can't pretend to be in some form of recovery, because I'm not, and I don't think I ever will be. I'm managing Bipolar and it will always be a part of who I am. I don't intend to recover from Bipolar, because it's just not an option. This is an illness that I'll have for life. It's severe and chronic, and I've had to accept that. It's part of my life. I can be miserable and hate the fact, or I can learn about it, start to understand the illness and find ways to manage it.

HOW DO I STAY STABLE?

That's the aim, isn't it? Getting to a stable place and being there for the foreseeable future. The dream, the major goal, the ultimate middle finger to mental illness. But it takes effort, discipline and a whole lot of looking after yourself.

- **Take your medication.** That is, if you've decided meds are the right avenue for you. If they are, and they're essential for many to reach stability, keep taking them even when you are stable. Don't lower the dosage or stop taking them altogether without speaking to your psychiatrist. It can cause horrible withdrawal, or you can become ill very quickly. It can be a huge temptation to throw all your medication away, either because you feel better and have done for some time or because you miss certain Bipolar symptoms. Talk to your psychiatrist about slowly reducing your dosage if you feel you can manage that. There's also no shame in going back to medication in the future – we all need an extra helping hand now and again. It doesn't mean you've failed; it actually means you're taking charge of your illness and being mature enough to realize you need help. However, some people will take medication long-term, or even for the rest of their lives. Again, no shame attached. Whatever works for you. Go with it, if it keeps you stable.
- **Go to therapy.** This might be just at the beginning

of your diagnosis, or something you want to carry on with in the long term. It might depend on what you think the root cause of Bipolar is for you. If you've been through childhood trauma, for instance, you may want to seek therapy specifically for that. Therapy can give us a better understanding of the condition, and help us identify our triggers. If you find it difficult to identify these, therapy could help you see patterns you've never noticed before. Talking it through can help you come to terms with and accept your diagnosis and deal with any guilt, anger or sadness you have about it.

- **Look out for big events and stressors.** Plan, plan and plan some more. Really, plan. I mean it. Schedule time out before, during and after an event. Identify something that you know is going to cause you stress and do something about it. This might be talking it through with someone or putting things in place with your partner, family, friends or manager at work that will help you to cope.

- **Avoid triggers.** Well, as much as you possibly can. If it's alcohol, sobriety might be a step you need to take. Obviously, it depends on each individual. You might just want to cut back. Have a sleep routine, eat healthily, get some exercise and generally just look after yourself. It can feel a bit dull at times, but would you trade feeling well for the tumultuous life you had before? I wouldn't. It also means you can do things you might have turned down before, because you've been too unwell.

- **Find a therapeutic outlet.** We all have a hobby or an interest. These might change over time, or we might find new ones. They can be integral to staying stable.

You don't have to be good at it! If it keeps you on an even keel, then that's what's important. For instance, I love painting. I'm not the best at it, and there will be times I'll just paint whatever, without a plan in mind. I'll finish painting and wonder what the hell I was thinking! It's not about the end product, but the process.

- **Know your limits.** It's like knowing what your kryptonite is. We all have a limit that will push us into an episode of depression or hypomania/mania. It might be taking on too much in our personal lives, whether it's other people's problems or going out too much. Learn to be selfish. Yeah, I meant what I said. There's absolutely nothing wrong with being selfish to look after our wellbeing. Sometimes we need to take a holiday from worrying about other people. Being selfish doesn't always mean we're hurting the people we care about; it means focusing on ourselves. This gives us the strength to be there for the people we care about. Recognize when you need 'me time', and learn to say no to people. It's good to set boundaries with others that can be unspoken, but you're aware of them.

- **Recognize behaviours.** Learn to recognize your warning behaviours, such as irritability, inability to concentrate and a lack of motivation. When you notice these, it's time to go on red alert. Talk to a doctor or psychiatrist, make a therapy appointment or use some of the suggestions from this list. You want to tackle these behaviours as soon as possible. It might be nothing to worry about, but it's always good to have some self-awareness.

- **Celebrate your achievements.** They can be as small as getting a good night's sleep, or they might be something bigger, like earning a promotion. It's all about allowing ourselves to feel pride in something we've achieved. It also celebrates what stability has brought us. One way we can do this is writing a note every time we achieve something when we're stable, big or small. Get a jar and pop the note in, and watch the jar fill up. When you're doubting what stability has done for you, empty the jar and read your notes. It will put everything in perspective and give you the lift and motivation to keep going.

- **Take care of your finances.** Overspending in hypomania or mania can have far-reaching and devastating consequences. People with Bipolar have lost their homes, been declared bankrupt and been trapped in persistent debt. Those financial stresses can even cause a mood episode. When you're stable, it's a chance to tackle some of that debt. Look for better interest rates on credit cards and loans you might have taken out. Try to build up your savings if you can. Savings can then act as a 'buffer' for the future, just in case you become ill again and can't work. Instal a site blocker on your computer and phone. When you've recognized the warning signs for an episode of mania or hypomania, block the websites you spend the most money on. Pick a random password and give it to a person you trust.

- **Reach out to communities online and off.** Support groups are a life saver for many people with Bipolar. They show you you're not alone. Even when we're stable, they can be a source of comfort. If you're struggling with the idea of being stable, groups give you a chance to voice these worries. I'm deeply connected to my online world and the connections I continue to create.

There's been a refocus in my online life in the past three years, to Twitter and the mental health community on the site. Twitter can be an endlessly supportive place; it's just the way you use it that's important. I've managed to find a group of people on whom I can rely when life gets tough.

HAVE A CRISIS PLAN

Part of managing Bipolar is planning for a crisis. Even when we're stable and managing well, it's always a good idea to plan for the future. I'll be real, though; the idea can be difficult. Planning for something you hope won't happen doesn't feel anything like a good time, although it will help you think about what you want to happen if you become very ill, and the support you'll need. There are a number of things you can do for yourself before a crisis hits:

- Talk to your doctor about options for treatment and support.
- Find details of helplines and listening services. Write them down for later, including numbers and when they're open (see the end of this book).
- Get involved with peer support. Talking to people with similar experiences will give you tips and advice to try.
- Make a self-care box. Fill a box with distractions or things you find comforting. Make one up in advance, because it's really difficult to come up with ideas in a crisis. Use apps such as *Stay Alive* to help you plan ideas.

Planning in advance helps you personalize what works for you. It means you'll have help and support before a crisis starts.

MAKING PLANS WITH FRIENDS AND FAMILY

Informally plan with people close to you how you want to manage a crisis. It helps to plan for the future and enables family and friends to understand that although you're stable, there is a chance you could have a crisis. Write down what you've all decided. Then you can remember what everyone has suggested and agreed on:

- How they can help you spot the warning signs of a crisis.
- How you want them to help.
- Who they should contact if you're unable to.
- What treatment you'd prefer, such as not wanting to be hospitalized.

You might want a family member to act as your advocate. It's frustrating when people aren't listening to us. With Bipolar, it can be hard to get people to listen to us, have our opinions heard and be taken seriously. An advocate supports you and helps you to express your views and wishes, and to stand up for your rights. They can listen to your concerns, help you research your rights and help you contact people, or contact them on your behalf. They can come along with you and support you in meetings and appointments, which can be stressful when you're very ill. Here they can:

- make sure all points are covered
- support you to ask questions
- explain your options
- keep you safe, ensuring you take regular breaks.

MAKE AN ADVANCE STATEMENT

When you're very ill, you might become unable to make decisions about your treatment. This is called losing capacity. An advance statement is a written statement about what you'd like to happen if you lose capacity. You can ask your doctor, care co-ordinator, psychiatrist or other healthcare professional to help you with this. What should you include in an advance statement?

- Your treatment preference, so where you'd like to be cared for, such as home or hospital.
- How you'd like a religious or spiritual belief to be reflected in your care.
- How you like to do things, such as if you prefer baths or showers.
- Things you like, such as a scent, being outside or inside, favourite foods.
- Who you'd like to look after your children or pets.
- Who you would like to deal with your benefits and bills.
- What happens when you become unwell.
- What treatment you would refuse.

It must be signed by you and a witness. Tell your doctor or mental health team you have an advance statement – you can even give them a copy for your records. You could also update a health app on your phone to show you have an advance statement. A statement like this isn't legally binding, but you could make an advance decision, which is similar in terms of setting out what your wishes are, but will need to be signed by you and a witness and *is* legally binding. With this you can refuse certain types of health care and treatment.

A crisis card is a small card you can carry in your wallet, purse or pocket. It'll have key details of how you'd like to be helped in a crisis. You can tell people you trust about the card and where you keep it.

Make decisions about what works for you and what doesn't. Everyone is different and, of course, different things work for different people.

SO YOU'RE STABLE, BUT WHAT IF YOU DON'T ACTUALLY LIKE IT?

It can be a strange situation. It's one you might not have experienced for years. It's called stability. Life can feel full of desperate lows and extreme highs, and not much in between. It's true you've had short periods of stability. However, this time it's different.

It can feel strange and alien to be stable. We're used to living an intense life, full of drama, fear, anger, emotional heights and depths. The euphoria you feel during a manic episode is unparalleled by any other you've experienced. I've experimented with drugs in the past, but nothing comes close to a full bout of mania. I say I don't need to take hallucinogens either because psychosis has that covered.

Back to life being surreal when you're stable. You won't be used to it. It feels different to be calm and organized. To feel happiness without worrying it'll morph into something toxic. Or to have days when you wake up and feel slightly on the down side, but able to carry on without depression creeping up on you. You finally feel as if you can accomplish things, without obsessing over a task and becoming completely absorbed by it. You start wondering if this is normality, or if there is such a thing. Is this how healthy people live?

It can be easy to daydream about the fun side of hypomania or mania. It can be easy to fall into the trap of stopping all your medications to get back to it. I say you should smash those rose-tinted glasses. Life definitely wasn't better before stability. Think back to what the highs were really like. The messed-up relationships. The intense anger, the overspending and the obsessive and dangerous behaviour. There's also that air of foreboding surrounding you that at any time you could become seriously ill again.

You might not always be sure you like this feeling. Life might feel quite bland and monotonous, at first. It can feel as if the world is slightly overcast and grey, instead of full of darkness or bright sunlight. But you know what? *That's what life should be like.* It's not always dramatic or intense. It feels a bit of a cliché to say so, but sometimes it's just about living through each day. It's a new way of living, and you can adjust. Life shouldn't constantly be full of extremes. It should be quieter. Sometimes, yes, it should even be boring.

BIPOLAR LESSONS

Over the years since my diagnosis, I've had a chance to absorb and process what this means to me. It all explained my manic, self-destructive behaviour. I've realized that stress is the number-one trigger for manic episodes. Stress in my personal life and at work culminates in a flurry of creative activity, incessant talking and obsessive, intense behaviour that no one can redirect me from. Then the inevitable crash into desperation at the crushing depression I suddenly experience.

Having a routine and sticking to it is paramount. Routine is my bestie. During the week, I go to bed at the same time every night, and have an alarm to get up each morning. I have an alarm every evening to take my medication. Sitting down every evening and planning what I'm going to do the next day gives me purpose when I'm depressed, and stops me from over-exerting myself when I'm on the cusp of mania.

I've never been very good at putting myself first. I am by nature a caring person and have a need to help others. I've realized that I've been dismissive of my own feelings. Being as ill as I have, I've had to be a bit more selfish in order to start getting better. It's always been easier to sort out other people's problems rather than face up to my own. Before anything, I need to be on a level kilter. I need to help myself first. Knowing I have to live for the rest of my life with this diagnosis means my health now outweighs other aspects of my life. This was a scary realization. My work and looking out for others has always played a part in my life. It still can, but I have to manage my health before helping others.

I've been so wrapped up in learning to manage Bipolar that I hadn't looked at how these extreme ups and downs had been affecting those closest to me. I know I can be difficult to be around sometimes and that my moods can be very unpredictable. This isn't easy for my family and husband, who I know sometimes feel as if they have to walk on eggshells around me. I'm trying to be more mindful of my changing moods. I often feel guilty for being unwell and that I'm a burden and a strain on my loved ones. Well, yes, I can be. Now, though, I'm at the point where I know nobody resents me for this. I've been as open and honest as I can with the people closest to me.

I often find it easier to write down my feelings than articulate them. I blog regularly. It's become a therapeutic experience. It's an outlet to express the feelings I can't vocalize but need people to understand. My husband and family have told me they now have a greater understanding of Bipolar from reading my blog. This has only strengthened our relationships. My husband and family are now more confident in how they can support me.

I'm accepting that it isn't selfish to want to be healthy. That I can't always be responsible for my erratic behaviour. However, I can become more aware and explain it to others. My family, friends and husband love me unequivocally, regardless of my health. I can't change my illness and it can be incredibly draining to hide from others. I've resolved not to paint the mask on, no matter how difficult it may be.

SELF-HONESTY

Honesty. A subject I harp on about often. I like to think I'm an honest, upfront individual and that this is reciprocated by the people around me. It's about mutual respect – if I'm honest and open with you, then I should expect the same in return. However, there's something that evades me: self-honesty. I'm not always honest with what is going on within my own mind. Often we creep around an emotion for fear that if we face it, we'll become engulfed by it. It's not a healthy attitude to have when you suffer from Bipolar.

A few years ago, I was in the middle of a severe bout of depression. It was one of the longest stretches of time I'd felt so low. Everyone has had that moment when you *need* to cry – whether it's because of physical pain, grief, loss, a break-up or just a ridiculously sh***y day. So you scream, cry and sob but then afterwards you feel a release. You feel better, more restored and ready to face life's next challenge. Engaging with that raw emotion and facing up to it is what allows us to carry on during difficult circumstances.

Looking back to that point, I found it immensely difficult to cry. That sounds strange, coming from a person who has faced up to the fact they are depressed. I've made excuses for myself:

that I'm a strong person and I don't need to cry. Blaming the medication for dampening down emotions. The people around me won't want to see a blubbering wreck. Even that crying is self-indulgent. But these are all lies. I'd been lying to myself and denying a healthy response to my ill-health.

I couldn't cry; something was holding me back that I didn't want to recognize. I was scared to cry, to have that release. If I cried, I would break that barrier. I would be out of control and unsure of what I would do to myself. I wanted to be strong and not give in to depression. It culminated at Christmas when I could no longer bottle up how awful I really felt. The tears flowed, and along with them the negative, painful emotions I'd suppressed.

I'm slowly realizing I need to take my own advice – face a problem head on, be honest with myself about the emotions I'm feeling and face up to them. It'll be painful, but I will heal faster and gain more self-awareness.

ARE YOU DEFINED BY BIPOLAR?

Mental illness plays a major part in my life. I talk about it often. I do this because I'm desperate to raise awareness and for funding to be increased for mental health services. Both of these issues drag behind those for physical health. It's unfair and discriminatory, so I feel it's my duty to speak out on behalf of those who are unable to. This doesn't mean I'm defined by the illness I suffer from. I admit, there isn't a day that goes by where I don't think about it; I have to, in order to stay stable and healthy.

I am so much more than my mental illness; I'm a geek, with a passion for video games, science fiction and anime. Currently, I'm writing a fiction novel and I love to create, whether it's sculpting, sketching or painting. I'm a vegan, and every time I see a picture of a polar bear, I cry (I can't help it!). I believe in a fairer society for all. I taught myself throat singing.

When a friend or family member speaks out about a mental illness they are suffering from, they need to be treated as they were before they said anything. Their illness isn't the only topic of conversation you can speak to them about from now on. They are a person with an identity, personality, hopes and dreams, hobbies and passions. They are not just 'the poorly one' or 'the awkward one', or even 'the weird one' or the one you stopped speaking to because you didn't know what to say or how to deal with it.

Learning and educating yourself about a condition can be freeing. You realize it can be managed and that it doesn't need to consume your life. You are more than your mental illness. When you invite others to share your knowledge, it gives them an opportunity to see past the illness to the real person behind it.

BREAK THE SILENCE

Too many people with Bipolar are silent. Silent with friends and family, silent at work, silent from their doctors, and silent from themselves. Breaking that silence can feel like the hardest thing in the world. When you break the silence surrounding Bipolar, it's freeing and empowering. To finally share your story with someone, even if it's just one person, can come as a huge relief. Sharing your struggles lifts a weight off your shoulders and has a positive effect that staying silent will never give you.

However, not everyone with Bipolar feels capable of being open. We share our stories, to varying degrees, with select people.

We don't all need to put ourselves 'out there'. I'm fully aware of how open I am (sometimes I cringe at how much), and hey, if sharing this book with someone is your way, if telling one person about your story is your way, that's OK too. If going out and seeking help and support is your way, then I'm celebrating that fact with you! I'll bring the cake. We're all different, despite our shared illness. Breaking the silence means talking as much or as little as you want to. It isn't a competition. No one should feel pressured to tell *everyone* they meet about their illness. Do what's right for you, and you'll find it makes a difference not only to your life but also to the people you care about.

Keep talking – whether it's relatable or not. It's not an easy subject to talk about. Even starting a conversation about Bipolar can feel awkward and daunting. It can feel jarring to suddenly start talking about it. It's an alien topic for people who haven't experienced it. Sometimes it feels as if you have to judge the atmosphere and the mood of the person you're talking to. If it's badly timed, it can shock a person and even distance them from you. The reaction could be silence. It could be that they completely ignore what you've said and change the subject. Sometimes you can see the fear of what to say next in a person's eyes. Really, it's about truthfully communicating and educating others. I'll ask them:

'What is it about Bipolar that scares or worries you?'

Or:

'Why does this conversation make you feel uncomfortable?'

If I just let it slide, I'll never know the answer.

BREAK UP WITH BIPOLAR

Is Bipolar your BFF? Bipolar can overwhelm us at times. It can dictate our decisions, affect our relationships and stop us from doing the things we enjoy. Urgh. Sometimes, though, Bipolar becomes more than just an illness; it becomes our life. Or, to put it another way, our best friend.

It's weird how Bipolar distorts our thinking, how it morphs into something that becomes so central in our lives. It becomes our friend. A constant companion that we take with us everywhere we go. It comes along to parties, family events, school or work. It's not silent either; it whispers in our ears and tells us we're not loved, we're not capable. It wants to be our best friend, our only friend.

The problem when Bipolar is your BFF is how much control it has over you. It'll distract you from what you want to do. It will distance you from family and friends. It wants you to be alone – that's its goal. So now all you have is it – the illness. It can completely take over your life if you allow it.

It's important to recognize when this is happening. I talk about Bipolar, a lot. I do so because I want to be open about it, and make it a less taboo thing to talk about. When I talk about how I'm feeling in a negative inward-looking way, I need to think about my actions. Am I overthinking, becoming paranoid and fixating on how I'm feeling? Is this encouraging Bipolar to become more central in my life? When this happens, I have to stop myself and gain some self-awareness.

No one really wants to be ill. We want to be healthy and stable. But sometimes Bipolar plays tricks on us. It makes us believe we're deserving of it, and this feeds our relationship with it. We're all worthy of a best friend – a real one, who supports and encourages us, and one that can tell us we're loved when Bipolar is telling us the opposite.

CHAPTER 9

HOW CAN I HELP?

Practical Tips for Family, Friends and Caregivers

This chapter is intended for family, friends and caregivers. Share it with your loved ones and encourage them to read it.

Starting the conversation about Bipolar can feel overwhelming, but it doesn't have to be. Someone struggling may only need the smallest gesture to pull them through. You have the tools to help them, even if you don't realize it.

Helping or caring for someone involves a number of ways you support them. Just because you don't physically take care of them doesn't mean it's any less draining, or that it's not hard work. There are a number of ways you can help a loved one with Bipolar disorder:

- Give them emotional support.
- Make sure they are safe.
- Encourage and help them to seek help.
- Help them cope with and accept the diagnosis.
- Encourage other family and friends to help.

- Help other family and friends to understand Bipolar disorder.
- Offer to go to appointments or advocate for them.
- Remind them to take medication.
- Cook and clean for them.
- Help them budget and look after their finances.

First up, it's all about how to spot the signs. You might find it easier to notice when they're depressed, or when they're hypomanic or manic. It depends on how much their behaviour changes. The signs you spot may overlap, so it might be difficult at first to understand what kind of mood episode they're at risk of. There are some signs that they might be leaning towards depression:

- change in how they act
- more withdrawn
- irritable
- less productive
- time taken off work or school unexpectedly
- less motivation
- loss of interest in social activities or hobbies
- change in appearance/not looking after themselves
- change in appetite.

For hypomania/mania:

- again, change in how they act, including acting erratically
- more risk taking
- change in appetite
- change in appearance
- sleeping less

- lack in concentration
- irritability
- fast, pressured speech.

Don't beat yourself up for missing the signs. The main thing is being there for them when they're ill. Bipolar is still an illness. Talk to them about these signs and explore together what their signs for an episode might be. If you've noticed certain behaviours, don't be afraid to let them know. It could help you both to spot depression, hypomania or mania in the future. Along with the warning signs, it's important to understand and recognize their triggers. You can talk together about how you can help manage these triggers or how to avoid them altogether.

Seeing someone unwell with Bipolar, or any illness for that matter, we have a tendency to want that person to be better as soon as possible. Our intentions, although coming from a good and caring place, are not always helpful.

I must stress here that jumping to conclusions is not a good thing when it comes to Bipolar. Caring for someone with Bipolar isn't easy and can be emotionally draining. It's especially so if you're constantly worrying and looking out for warning signs. Being this on edge is not good for your health, or the best way to support your loved one. Don't assume a sudden change in mood is a sign of an episode. We all know from our experiences that it's possible to feel a range of emotions but still be mostly stable. One behaviour that's out of character in isolation isn't always a sign that we should be planning for a full-blown crisis. You need to give the person with Bipolar some credit too. Trust them to know their triggers and warning signs, rather than second-guessing every behaviour and mood change you see. It's about striking a balance, and the best way to find this balance? Talk to each other.

WHAT SHOULD I SAY?

What family, friends and caregivers can do is acknowledge their loved one's difficulties with Bipolar. Really listening to how it affects them, reading literature and going to support groups can all help you understand Bipolar that little bit better. Making simple statements to them about Bipolar can make them feel that they've been listened to and, more importantly, understood. Listen, and then interpret what they've said in your own words. There are a number of ways you can word your responses: it doesn't have to be complicated or scientific, and you don't have to prove to them how much you know about the condition – that isn't the point. The point is them feeling that you've heard them, because everyone who has Bipolar has a unique perspective and struggles more with certain symptoms. Be open to talking to them about their experiences. This will help them feel supported and accepted by you. You could say:

'So what you're saying is...'

'I can see you're struggling.'

'Feeling depressed and hopeless must be so difficult for you.'

'It must be tough feeling so irritable and restless.'

What they need to hear is you just acknowledging their difficulties. Knowing you'll be there for them is important. You don't need to try to fix them. Stability is the goal for everyone with Bipolar, but that comes in time. It can't be magically achieved overnight. It's a long process that could take years. What someone with Bipolar needs from you is to just be there for them, and show your love and support. You can do this by accepting the illness and being alongside them while they try to navigate it.

My partner, Jimi, has this to say about living with and maintaining a relationship with someone with Bipolar:

'From a partner's perspective, I can't stress enough that communication is key. If you think things are a bit too good or a bit too down, don't be afraid to ask if they're OK. I spent a long time giving in to what I now know were the beginnings of mania or hypomania. I felt like I'd be a buzz-kill if I asked that and it turned out to just be normal excitement over something. I now question "Let's go out and get drunk", no matter how tempting it may be! Yes, this does mean that sometimes I question normal behaviour, but I'd rather do that than miss something important.

It's important to talk about libido. Particularly before stability happened, things were up and down. Libido could be very down for weeks, or very up for weeks. This was either awesome or challenging to deal with. Particularly during the downtimes, I found myself asking if it's me. Talking about this is crucial.

I've learned to question medication. Have you taken your meds? Are you going to take your meds? I've paused films and refused to press play until meds have been taken, because we've reached that time and I didn't want us to forget! Yeah, I'm annoying sometimes, but I don't care if it gets the medication taken!

I could try to think of more examples, but they would all echo the same theme. Communicate, communicate, communicate!'

IF YOU'RE WORRIED FOR SOMEONE'S WELLBEING, HOW DO YOU GO ABOUT SUPPORTING THEM?

- **Ask them how they're doing.** Simple, right? If you

have an inkling something isn't right, *really* ask them if they're OK, as if you mean it. You're not hoping and wishing for a simple 'I'm fine'. Talk to them in a relaxed atmosphere, or over a drink. Go for a walk together. Mention your concerns and the changes you've noticed.

- **Ring or message if you haven't heard from them for a while.** It could mean they're struggling and have isolated themselves. Knowing that someone is thinking of them could be what starts them talking.

- **Tell them you're there to listen.** So they've started talking to you – what do you do now? Listen and give them space to talk freely. Listen attentively. Repeat back key phrases and sum up what they've told you in your own words. It'll show that you've heard and understood.

- **Share your own experiences.** Maybe you or someone else in your life has gone through a difficult time? Share that experience so they feel less alone.

- **Don't fall into the trap of making it all about you, or what you've been through.** Yes, share your experiences, but not in a way that is dismissive of what your loved one is going through. This conversation is ultimately about them, how they're feeling, and you learning more about the condition.

CONVERSATION STARTERS

'I've noticed you've been less talkative recently. Is there anything worrying you?'

'I've noticed you've not been yourself recently. Is there anything you want to talk about?'

'I haven't heard from you for a while and I wanted to see if you needed any support with anything?'

'Is there anything I can do to help?'

'Do you want to go for a coffee and a chat about how you're doing?'

'I'm always here if you need to talk.'

WHAT CAN I DO TO HELP?

You don't need to fix them. Someone feeling that they're in a desperate place doesn't need to be told to 'take a bath', 'go for a run' or 'drink some camomile tea'. We as human beings want to fix problems and sometimes we can't fix them completely. If you're not a medical professional, then being there, talking to them and listening are the best things you can do.

My Mum has struggled with wanting to 'fix' me, but has learned, with time, how best to support me:

'Being a Mum and having a daughter with Bipolar has been challenging! As a Mum, you want your child to be happy, healthy, enjoying life, not shutting themselves away, with mood swings, erratic behaviour, anger and sadness. That was my daughter for many years and I did not know or understand what was wrong. When my daughter was diagnosed with Bipolar in 2012, in some ways it was a relief. After years of struggling with her mood swings and erratic behaviour, at last we had an answer.

This was just the start of life with our daughter and her

diagnosis. I remember being really careful about what I said to her, how I said things, and I felt as if I was walking on eggshells. I really did not know how to deal with this. I started to attend a Bipolar support group with my daughter, which made me realize that she was still my daughter, she just had Bipolar.

The most difficult times are when she is ill and really struggling with every aspect of life. All I want to do is make her better and make this awful thing inside her go away. I have learned that the best way I can help is in a practical way, helping with the chores in the house, communicating with her and her husband and being honest, and most of all telling her she is special and loved.

I have learned not to walk on eggshells. My relationship with my daughter has changed for the better; we are open and honest with each other, and I am no longer worried about saying things that might upset her or make her angry. Katie is still Katie, my beautiful, clever, amazing, passionate, kind and caring daughter who has Bipolar.'

WITH ALL THAT IN MIND, WHAT PRACTICAL SUPPORT CAN YOU OFFER?

- **Help them write down questions.** If they need to go to appointments, benefit hearings, for instance, writing a list together of what they would like to say will help them. If they're struggling, their thoughts could be all over the place and jumbled. Organize the list for them so the most important points are at the top.
- **Organize their paperwork with them.** Make sure bills, letters from their doctors, important notes they've made about treatment, and prescriptions are all kept in an accessible, safe place. Divide their paperwork into

categories, so it's easier to find what they need and keep on track with bills.

- **Help with practical tasks.** This includes things such as taking them food shopping, helping or arranging childcare, doing household cleaning and other daily jobs. You could offer them a lift to appointments or join them on public transport if they're feeling nervous or anxious.

- **Accompany them to the appointments.** In addition to taking them to appointments, it's often a good idea to go with them to the actual appointment. I've found this immensely helpful. Even with notes I've made, I sometimes forget to mention something vital. I might feel too overwhelmed to fully articulate how I'm feeling. Having someone who knows me sitting there provides me with emotional support. It's also helpful for doctors and psychiatrists to hear an alternative view. Your loved one may think everything is going along well, but you've noticed things aren't quite right. It helps to tell a medical professional your concerns to put your mind at ease, and to make sure the loved one you're with is getting the correct treatment.

- **Do your own research.** Looking up information about Bipolar and treatment options not only helps the person with the condition, but helps you understand and support them. Gather information and sit down with them and have a chat about all their options. Talking it through can help them decide what will work for them.

My Dad explains what it's been like having a daughter with Bipolar disorder, and the lessons he's learned:

'When Katie was born and for the first two years of her life, she was my little angel and as a Dad I was so proud of her, and still am. At around two years old, Katie's personality started to change and to be honest I thought it was great because I always wanted the children to grow up as independent as they could be.

When our youngest son Tom was born, Katie was six years old and he had some additional needs which took up a lot of our time as parents. At the same time, we were foster carers and put a lot of effort into helping young people experience a real family. In hindsight, I think Katie got a bit lost, being a middle child and helping a lot with the foster children we had to stay. I didn't pay much attention. I thought she was just quiet, but when I look back, I believe she was withdrawing.

When she moved to secondary school, it was then I began to notice she was different, but even then that wasn't a problem for me, because I value difference in people and still do. Katie made it through school and came out with good qualifications to enable her to access a creative writing course at university. I was so pleased for her and fully supportive because I knew how creative she was with words and art. Katie found university difficult and I still don't know the full story behind her deciding it wasn't for her. I remember collecting her and thinking, what's next? Katie came home and we supported her as much as we could. She experienced some real issues with her mental health, including severe panic attacks which culminated in an ambulance being called. When Katie was diagnosed with Bipolar disorder, it was a shock but also a relief because it explained some of her "differences". It took me some time to understand that you can't just snap out of it or "cheer up" – it goes deeper than that. To help Katie, I have had to educate myself, but fundamentally I try, and I know it's a cliché, to be there for her through the ups and downs. Finally, I just try and tell her what a wonderful creative, caring person she is and how proud I am as a father.'

HOW CAN I HELP WHEN THEY'RE DEPRESSED?

Try not to be too critical. They haven't asked to be depressed, and they can't help how low they feel. They can't snap out of it, or just pull themselves together. If you've never experienced depression before, it can be easy to feel that way and get frustrated. Criticizing them won't help, and they're probably already feeling pretty sh***y about themselves. Pressuring them can make them feel even lower, and isolated and worthless.

You don't need to do everything for them. When you see someone deep in the throes of depression, it's easy to feel you need to take over. Of course, everyone needs different levels of support, but for both of you it's important they don't become completely reliant on you. Encourage them to help themselves; it might be cleaning the house with them, or buying them groceries so they can cook a healthy meal. Talk to them about the kind of help they need, and identify what they feel capable of.

Often someone doesn't want sympathy, and just knowing you're there for them if they need you is enough. You don't always need to find a solution – just keeping in touch and listening is worthwhile.

When someone is suicidal, they might suddenly seem calm and almost happy. This is a big warning sign that they have a plan to end their life. If someone you care about has been deeply depressed, but it seems that overnight they've recovered, it's vital you keep a close eye on them. When a person is suicidal, and have planned how, when and where they are going to take their life, it can feel to them at the time like a release. They'll feel almost relieved that they've made a decision and know when it's going to happen. If a loved one ever tells you they have a plan in place, seems preoccupied with death or starts making arrangements for when they're no longer here, they need support urgently.

WHAT ABOUT IF THEY'RE EXPERIENCING PSYCHOSIS?

The number-one thing you should do is to stay calm and speak to them gently. Don't panic. Make them feel at ease and comfortable to share what's going on. It's easy to get frustrated with someone when what they're saying doesn't make any sense. You might feel like calling them out and confronting them. Don't. What they're experiencing is very real to them in that moment. Challenging their beliefs could easily push them away, and if they're paranoid, it could even fuel the delusion. If you can encourage them to open up, then you're in a better position to help. It will show you if they're at risk of harming or endangering themselves. Make sure you listen and try to understand as best you can. You don't have to agree with what they're saying. You don't have to completely get it, especially if it doesn't make sense. Don't encourage a delusion as this can make things worse.

Focus on their feelings. Instead of focusing on what they're describing and saying, talk about how they feel. If they're angry, sad, worried, scared, frustrated or paranoid, focus on the specific emotion. It can be easy to get caught up in and swept away by what they are saying. You may find yourself correcting or arguing with them. This won't achieve anything. You can't prove to them the delusion isn't true, because they are not in the right frame of mind to listen to reason and logic. Instead, make them feel safe and secure, which can help guide them through the experience.

Show them respect. Don't be critical of what they're going through, or over-protective. You might feel that you know better, and telling them what to do will help. However, it often creates a divide. You can respect their wishes to an extent. For instance, if they want to be supported at home, rather than in hospital, you should respect that, unless they become a danger to themselves or others. Empathizing with them is another way to show you care and understand. If they're hearing or seeing something that's troubling them, tell them how it would make you feel if you were going through it. If you can put yourself in their shoes, they will feel less alone.

Lastly, ask them simply if you can help. They might feel afraid to leave the house, or that what they're experiencing is too overwhelming and they can't complete everyday tasks. I find that during a psychotic episode, it can feel as if nothing else matters, so I find it hard to look after myself. Ask them if you can pick up some shopping for them or cook them a meal. Remind them that it's important to sleep, eat and take a shower. It could be as simple as giving them your full attention and listening to their thoughts.

Helpful things to say include:

'It must be so scary to hear shouting in your head.'

'You seem to be managing OK, but is there anything I can do to help?'

'I don't know what to make of what you're saying. It's so confusing and upsetting to hear everything you're telling me. You seem to be handling it very well, though.'

WHAT DO I DO WHEN THEY'RE MANIC OR HYPOMANIC?
The best way to tackle this is by making a plan before an episode starts. When they're feeling well, they will be more receptive to

ideas. When someone is stable, they have more control and will be able to look objectively at their hypomania or mania. You could look at their work commitments and any other projects they have and offer your own opinion on them. Maybe you feel they've taken on too much, which could lead to stress and burnout, which could then lead to an episode. Be calm and gentle with the suggestion, so they don't feel you're being overly protective or critical. Again, to keep them healthy, you could help them stick to a routine. Making sure they have regular meals and a sleep routine will help to keep them well, or to be in a healthier place when the hypomania or mania ends.

During an episode, you could do things together with them. If they are being creative, join in. It shows you're interested in what they're up to, and means you can set boundaries for how long they spend on the activity. Again, don't force them to stop, but remind them of other things they need to do that day, or that they need to eat, sleep and look after themselves. You might have to manage their money when they are unwell. This can be organized beforehand, doing things such as putting a site blocker on their phone or computer that only you know the password to. It'll stop them from spending money on websites you know they use often. You may need to take their cards from them and have access to their bank account. If they need money for something, they will then have to ask you. It might feel as if you're infantilizing them, but believe me, they will appreciate it when they are stable.

THE DIFFICULT STUFF

Sometimes when someone is very ill, their behaviour can be challenging. It's difficult to understand and to deal with. Often when someone is manic or hypomanic, they can be very disinhibited. Their behaviour could be embarrassing for you. It might be strange and they act oddly around you and others. It could even be upsetting or aggressive. It's important that you talk about this and don't let it fester. It probably isn't the best time to talk to them right there and then, because in a manic or hypomanic state they might not listen to reason. Actually, they almost definitely won't. They won't be able to see your point of view. So it's best to wait until they're stable. Write down what you want to tell them, so you don't forget what it was they said or did. Writing it down can help you cope with your own feelings, without reaching boiling point. Calmly discuss how their behaviour, words or actions made you feel. Try not to judge or be overly critical. Remember that they were ill at the time, and would not have been aware of how much they upset or concerned you. Tell them how their actions and words made you feel. Don't generalize or accuse them of acting in a certain way; instead, turn it around and explain how you felt at the time.

If they're having hallucinations or delusions, they might feel angry, annoyed or confused with you for not understanding. Again, try to stay calm, even when their behaviour is difficult or their words are hurtful. Let them know that you don't share their beliefs or see or hear what they can, but that you understand it feels real for them.

You might feel frustrated and powerless. We all have our limits for what we're capable of managing and what we can do. There's also the problem that you might recognize they are ill before they do, and they might not admit they need help. They could push you away or say upsetting things. This is where the list of warning signs you made when they were stable comes in handy. It can make it easier to bring it up and talk about it.

If they are having distressing thoughts, they might take it

out on the people closest to them. You're allowed to be upset if they are pushing you away. Remember why they are acting that way: they are ill and dealing with difficult moods and emotions. When things start getting too difficult, it's OK to take time out. If you're worried what will happen if you need some time away, then ask friends and family to help out. It could help to talk to other people in a similar situation.

My older brother, James, explains how my challenging behaviour affected him:

'I'm Katie's brother and I'm a habitual "fixer". I'm the kind of person who sees a problem and wants to solve it, to provide a solution. From my experience, Bipolar doesn't vibe very well with this mindset. Bipolar definitely isn't something you can fix with a bit of advice or "have you tried this" suggestions. Because of this, having a close relationship with someone with Bipolar can be an immensely frustrating experience.

When my sister was first diagnosed with Bipolar, all I wanted to do was "fix" her. This caused frustration on both sides, and in hindsight my frustration was born out of a lack of understanding of what Bipolar is and how it affected my sister. I found it hard to tell where the Bipolar ended and Katie started, and this meant I didn't really know how to behave towards her at times. I ended up resenting the condition, which then led to me resenting her because I couldn't help her in the way I thought I should be able to. Essentially, it made me feel kind of helpless.

Over the last few years, I've begun to think differently about Katie and Bipolar. As I've learned more about the condition and my sister, I've stopped thinking about it in such a binary way and see Bipolar almost as a part of her identity. I've tried to stop always offering a fix or solution (not always successfully). I've realized the best help I can give is to make sure my sister knows I'm always around if she needs me and to just treat her like a normal person and not like someone "who is Bipolar".'

WHAT IF THEY DON'T WANT HELP?

Sometimes it's obvious when someone is clearly unwell, but they might not see it or might refuse to get help. You can't make someone get help, but you can be there for them. Forcing someone to talk to you and get help can be damaging to your relationship with them. If they're an adult, you can't make them do what they don't want to. Ultimately, they are responsible for their own actions and can make their own decisions. If you pressure someone into talking to you, it can make them feel uncomfortable or even confrontational. They'll be less likely to open up when they are ready to talk.

You can encourage them to seek help, but not force them to. Give them information about where to go and whom to call when they're ready to. Tell them that you are there for them and care about them. Tell them that you're worried, but you won't make them do anything they don't want to; it's their choice.

If you're extremely worried about someone, it's important you encourage them to find help. You can encourage them to ring their mental health team if they have one, make a doctor's appointment or go to accident and emergency. There are also a number of helplines they can ring if they're feeling overwhelmed.

LOOK AFTER YOURSELF

It can be draining to be there for someone struggling, so it's important to look after yourself and invest some time and energy in this. You need to stay well so that you can offer support. You need to be honest that it can be tough for you too. If you're not, you can find yourself resenting the person you're caring for. Just because someone is ill doesn't mean you can't be honest about your feelings. Talking it through can even help your relationship with that person.

Take a break. It's easy to feel overwhelmed when you're supporting a loved one with Bipolar. Taking time out for you can help you recharge your energy and feel less stressed and more refreshed. Talking about your feelings to someone you trust can help you feel supported. It might help to find connections with people who are going through a similar experience helping someone. As I've already said, it's important to have boundaries in place. There is only so much you can do, and the person you're helping also needs to take responsibility for their own illness. You have to be realistic about how much support, and how much of yourself, you can give. Most of the time, just being there and listening is enough. You don't have to be making grand gestures constantly in order to be useful.

Bipolar disorder is complex, severe and long-lasting. The lessons I've learned along the way have taught me to be a better version of myself. I've learned to:

- give myself a break
- understand that I can't control everything, and I don't need to be perfect
- manage the illness with a mixture of medication, therapy and lifestyle changes
- use self-awareness to stop an episode in its tracks
- lean on people when I need help
- cherish the friendships I've made and the close family I have

- communicate honestly and openly with my family and friends
- take responsibility for looking after myself and staying well.

RESOURCES AND HELPLINES

UK

Bipolar UK: www.bipolaruk.org; 07591 375544; info@bipolaruk.org; ecommunity: bipolaruk.org/ecommunity

Samaritans: www.samaritans.org; 116 123; jo@samaritans.org

Papyrus HopelineUK: https://papyrus-uk.org/hopelineuk; 0800 068 4141; pat@papyrus-uk.org

Mind: www.mind.org.uk; 0300 123 3393; info@mind.org.uk

USA

Depression and Bipolar Support Alliance: www.dbsalliance.org; 1 800 273 8255

International Bipolar Foundation: https://ibpf.org; 1 858 598 5967

National Alliance on Mental Illness: https://nami.org; 1 800 950 6264

Mental Health America: www.mhanational.org; 1 800 969 6642; Suicide crisis hotlines: 1 800 784 2433 (in crisis); 1 800 273 8255 (to talk)

REFERENCES

Ghaemi, S.N., Boiman, E.E. and Goodwin, F.K. (2000) 'Diagnosing Bipolar Disorder and the Effect of Antidepressants: A Naturalistic Study.' *Journal of Clinical Psychiatry*, 61(10), 804–808. Accessed on 03/06/20 at www.psychiatrist.com/JCP/article/Pages/2000/v61n10/v61n1013.aspx.

Goodwin, F. and Redfield-Jamison, K. (2007) *Manic-Depressive Illness: Bipolar Disorders and Recurrent Depression*. New York: Oxford University Press.

McManus, S., Bebbington, P., Jenkins, R. and Brugha, T. (eds) (2016) *Mental Health and Wellbeing in England: Adult Psychiatric Morbidity Survey 2014*. Leeds: NHS Digital.

National Centre for Mental Health (2017) *Bipolar Disorder, Pregnancy and Childbirth. Information for Women, Partners and Families*. Accessed on 12/12/19 at www.ncmh.info.

National Institute of Mental Health (2017) *Prevalence of Bipolar Disorder Among Adults*. Accessed on 02/02/20 at www.nimh.nih.gov/health/statistics/bipolar-disorder.shtml.

Time to Change (2015) *Attitudes to Mental Illness Research Report*. Accessed on 29/01/20 at www.time-to-change.org.uk/media-centre/responsible-reporting/violence-mental-health-problems.